Fat Fannies Fudge Factory

Fat Fannies Fudge Factory

by

Elaine Coleman

Illustrated by **Gayle Vancil**

Bolton Publishing LLC

Brady, Texas

Bolton Publishing LLC
Brady, Texas

Dedication

This book is dedicated to all the fudge lovers in my family. Thanks for trying all the recipes whether you knew it or not.

Acknowledgements

It is with great pleasure and a bent funny bone that I thank friends from long ago and those of today for the fun times we have all had and the fun times yet to come.

Fat Fannies was a work I enjoyed very much, mostly because the stories are like memories and I loved to try the new fudges. I love to make those around me laugh and this is the book to make people laugh.

Thanks go out to Sam, Gwench, Becca D., Robyn "Pup", my husband Jerry, and to Gayle Vancil who without her illustrations this book would not be so cute. There are grandkids, and family members too numerous to mention, but you know who you are who tried the fudge and ate it even after I told you what was in it. You are my troopers.

Introduction

FUDGE, Freda Fiddlestick, Frankenstein, the Lottery, and trouble. Freda Fiddlestick dreamed of a fudge factory. She traveled from town to town for several years trying out her fudge recipes on the residents in her path. The only problem was trouble followed Freda everywhere she went.

Her first factory flooded with fudge that refused to harden properly; she lost her investment and her home. Undeterred, Freda took her dead husband's old panel truck, revamped it into a home with a kitchen where she lived and cooked her fudgy treats. The repainted truck sported a sign, Frankenstein's Fudgy Treats. She uncovered an eight-track player in the garage and a tape with calliope music to attract her prospective taste testers. Instead of ice cream, she peddled her fudgy treats to the residents of her hometown. One afternoon someone suggested she take her fudge on the road. Freda took to the idea like a fudge covered cookie. She hit the road with Willie Nelson's song on her lips and Freda and her truck became good time friends, selling her fudgy treats. Each season found her in a new place, until she arrived in Sling Shot, a small border town.

Trouble followed Freda to Sling Shot, but she made the best of every situation. When Frankenstein died at the only red light in town, Freda knew Sling Shot was her destiny. Her escapades made for good reading in the *Sling Shot Gazette*. Each of the articles written about Freda and her mishaps became a matter of record. Thanks to the editor of the Gazette, a few of Freda's recipes appeared at the end of each story for good measure. The free advertisement did wonders for her business.

Frankenstein, now gold plated in front of the, Fat Fannies Fudge Factory, testifies to Freda's determination and serves as an advertisement for fudge and winning the lottery.

Freda and her Sling Shot friends now own the largest fudge factory in the United States -- thanks to Frankenstein, trouble, the lottery, and fudge.

Fat Fannies Fudge Factory
Table of Contents

Frankenstein Died

Freda Fiddlestick's beat up old hippie truck shimmied past the Sling Shot city limits sign, swerved across the yellow line twice and expired at the town's only traffic light.

"Giddy-up, Frankenstein! The light's green."

Frankenstein wheezed, and Freda's key twisting in the ignition summoned only coughs and protests. She jumped from the vehicle, ran to the front bumper, lifted the hood, and muttered, "Thought I told you I can't afford to get any more work done on you."

Honks and yells of protest reached her ears. In a flurry of animated moves, Freda directed traffic around her dead truck. Twisting and turning this way and that, the middle aged woman broke into a gyrating dance in the middle of Sling Shot's main street. Car wheels squalled to a halt as drivers watched the sequin-bedecked woman. Sling Shot would never be the same.

1

Freda heard a police car siren and saw a patrol car pull alongside the run-down truck. The woman officer pointed to the sign "Frankenstein's Fudge Treats," and shook her head.

"Trouble ma'am?"

Freda Fiddlestick opened the patrol car door, read the officer's name badge, and took hold of the Officer Babs's hand. She waltzed the officer to the truck. A new plan formulated while they danced. "Frankenstein died! We've got to have a funeral."

"Who is Frankenstein?" Babs tried to look inside the windows of the vehicle. "Where is he?"

"He's my truck."

Babs peered at Freda oddly. "Well, ma'am we can't have a funeral here. You gotta get this heap of junk off the road."

Freda slapped Babs on the back and laughed. "My sentiments exactly. How do you propose I get this done? Frankenstein is dead. He ain't moving anywhere."

Babs stared into space for a long moment. "What we need here are a couple of young men."

Freda grinned and whispered. "I've been needing young men for years."

Exasperated, Babs stepped in front of the traffic and blew on her whistle. Every vehicle within hearing distance stopped. She walked to a pickup with several men inside.

In her best authoritative voice, she spoke. "Joe, I'm confiscating your muscles." She flung open the door and took hold of his arm. "We have a situation here. I need to get this junk heap off the street. The lady will guide the vehicle while you boys push her to the curb. "She motioned to the others. "Come on. He can't do it alone."

"Yes, ma'am." The men jumped to do her bidding.

"Hallelujah, praise be to glory," Freda's voice rang out. "Thank you, God, for sending these wonderfully strong men to our aid. As soon as they get Frankenstein off the road, I will reward them with a batch of my homemade fudge." She turned to the men and winked. "You'd all like that, wouldn't you?"

Each man found himself on the receiving end of a fierce hug and pat on the back. She instructed them on how to push Frankenstein to the edge of the street. Her sequined blouse bounced with every move she made. Satisfied the men's hands were placed in the right position, she clamored into the driver's seat, pulled the gearshift into neutral and leaned out the door. "Okay, boys, grab a hunk of metal and growl."

Joe and his friends pushed, but Frankenstein didn't budge an inch.

"Come on, boys, I know you got more muscle than that. Growl louder when you push. I know it helps." Freda sat behind the wheel waiting for the truck to move. Nothing.

"Wonder what she has in this thing anyway?" Hank asked the others while he tried to see inside.

The others shrugged. "Must be full of fudge. Didn't you see the sign on the side?" They leaned and pushed again.

Officer Babs blew her whistle. "Let's get this done, fellows. Traffic is backing up and the Sling Shoters are getting restless."

"Yes, ma'am." Joe smiled sweetly at her.

Hank whispered to Jonsey, and a message passed to Joe.

"What? Well no wonder." Joe straightened from his pushing position, dusted his hands together, and started for the front of the truck.

"What's the matter here?" Babs blew her whistle, but Joe kept walking. She skittered after him.

At the driver's door, Joe stopped and leaned on the open window. He peered inside where Freda sat and shook his head. "Ma'am, do you really want us to move this vehicle?"

"Well, of course, I do young man. By the way what is your name?" Freda fluttered her lashes.

"Joe, ma'am."

"I showed you how to push old Frankie to get him moving. Why are you out of place?" She started to get out of the truck.

Joe held the door closed. "Ma'am. We can't move you to the side of the street until..."

"Until what?"

"Until you get your foot off the brake!"

"Oh." Freda sheepishly lifted her foot from the brake.

Joe joined his friends at the tail of the vehicle. "Darn women drivers," he muttered.

Freda sat with her mouth open. Why hadn't she realized she had her foot on the brake? Red-faced, she sat back in the seat while the men pushed Frankenstein off the street.

The crowd cheered Joe and the others when they slowly rolled the vehicle to the curb. They began to disperse until loud calliope music filled the air. A ditty, belted out by none other than Freda followed. She held the microphone in one hand, and passed out various flavors of fruity homemade fudge with the other. The people milled about, muttering how good the fudge tasted. Freda listened carefully. She grinned so wide it was hard for her to keep singing.

Everyone knew who Freda Fiddlestick was and her fruity fudge was a hit. Just like she planned. All she needed was a new place to live and cook her confections. She wanted to try many more recipes, and the good folks of Sling Shot could be her guinea pigs. Her only regret, Frankenstein sat dead at the curb.

Apricot Nut Fudge

½ cup milk
1 ⅔ cups sugar
½ teaspoon salt
1 ½ cups marshmallows cut up
1 ½ cup chocolate chips
½ cup chopped pecans
½ cup chopped dried apricots

Mix milk, sugar, and salt in a pan and start it boiling. Cook about 5 minutes before removing from heat. Add remaining ingredients and stir until well blended. Pour into a buttered dish and cut into squares.

Chocolate Peach Fudge

3 cups sugar
¾ cup milk
3 tablespoons light corn syrup
¼ teaspoon salt
2 tablespoons butter
3 squares chocolate, unsweetened
1 teaspoon vanilla
3 fresh peaches chopped nuts

Combine in a pan, sugar, milk, chocolate, syrup, and salt. Boil until it reaches the soft ball stage. Pour cooked mixture into a large bowl immediately. Add butter and vanilla. Beat at a high speed until the mixture begins to cool and becomes creamy. Add peaches and nuts. Pour into a buttered pan.

Hawaiian Fudge

2 cups sugar
½ cup crushed pineapple, drained
½ cup thin cream
1 tablespoon butter
½ cup chopped pecans
Green food coloring

Mix everything together except the nuts and food coloring and bring to a boil. Cook until mixture reaches the soft ball stage. Add food coloring and beat until creamy and begins to thicken. Add nuts. Pour into buttered pan or dish to cool.

Chocolate Pineapple Fudge

1 cup milk
3 cups sugar
2 tablespoons butter
1 cup crushed pineapple drained
2 teaspoons lemon juice
3 squares melted German Chocolate

Mix together the milk, sugar, and butter. Heat on low until it boils. Add pineapple and chocolate, cooking to the soft ball stage. Stir so mixture does not stick. Cool the fudge and add lemon juice. Beat until mixture forms crystals. Turn it out into a buttered pan.

Papaya Fudge

1 ½ cup fresh ripe papaya cut from seed and mashed
½ teaspoon lemon flavoring
⅓ cup sweetened condensed milk
3 ½ cups sugar
½ cup water

Combine sugar, papaya, milk, and water. Cook to soft ball stage. Remove from heat and add the lemon flavoring. Cool for about 20 minutes. Beat until nice and creamy. Pour into buttered pans and let set for several hours. Cut into squares.

Key Lime Fudge

1 small package cream cheese
2 cups powdered sugar
½ cup key lime juice
¼ teaspoon vanilla
⅓ teaspoon salt
¾ cup chopped nuts

Cream the cheese with the sugar then add lime juice. Add vanilla, salt, and nuts, mixing thoroughly. Press into a buttered pan and cool in the refrigerator for about 15 minutes. If the fudge becomes too hard, add a teaspoon or so of cream when mixing in the vanilla and nuts.

Pumpkin Fudge

1 ½ cup canned pumpkin
½ teaspoon lemon flavoring
⅓ cup sweetened condensed milk
3 ½ cups sugar
½ cup water

Combine sugar, pumpkin, milk, and water. Cook to a soft ball stage. Remove from heat and add the lemon flavoring. Cool for about 20 minutes. Beat until nice and creamy. Pour into buttered pans and let set for several hours. Cut into squares.

Sweet Potato Fudge

1 ½ cup canned sweet potatoes
½ teaspoon lemon flavoring
⅓ cup sweetened condensed milk
3 ½ cups sugar
½ cup water

Mash the sweet potatoes and combine with sugar, milk, and water. Cook to a soft ball stage. Remove from heat and add the lemon flavoring. Cool for about 20 minutes. Beat until nice and creamy. Pour into buttered pans and allow to set for several hours. Cut into squares to serve.

Shore "Yam" Good Fudge

1 ½ cup grated yams
½ teaspoon lemon flavoring
⅓ cup sweetened condensed milk
3 ½ cups sugar
½ cup water

Combine sugar, yams, milk, and water. Cook to a soft ball stage. Remove from heat and add flavoring. Cool. Beat until nice and creamy. Pour into buttered pans to cool. Cut into squares.

Banana Cream Fudge

1 ½ cup mashed bananas
½ teaspoon lemon juice
⅓ cup sweetened condensed milk
3 ½ cups sugar
½ cup water
1 teaspoon vanilla

Combine sugar, bananas, milk, and water. Cook to a soft ball stage. Remove from heat and add lemon juice. Cool. Add vanilla. Beat until smooth and creamy. Pour into buttered pans and let set until hardened. Cut into squares.

Cherry Fudge

2 cups sugar
1 cup milk
1 tablespoon butter
¼ pound cherries

Mix sugar, milk, and butter. Bring to a boil. Cook about 8 minutes. Beat until creamy and add chopped cherries. Spread into buttered pan to cool.

White Cherry Fudge

2 ¼ cups sugar
½ cup sour cream
½ cup milk
2 tablespoons butter
1 tablespoon white corn syrup

¼ teaspoon salt
2 teaspoons vanilla
1 cup chopped pecans
½ cup chopped maraschino cherries

Combine all ingredients but the cherries, nuts, and vanilla. Cook until it boils. Bring it to the soft ball stage. Remove from heat and allow to cool until it is only slightly warm. Add vanilla, nuts, and cherries. Can be dropped on wax paper or put into a buttered pan and cut into squares.

Baked Fruit Fudge

2 tablespoons butter
1 cup sugar
2 eggs - separated
2 squares chocolate melted
1 teaspoon lemon extract
1 teaspoon orange extract

½ cup flour
1 teaspoon vanilla
½ cup each - dates, raisins,
figs, candied pineapple, and
cherries chopped

Cream the butter and sugar. Add egg yolks, melted chocolate, and extracts. Beat well, Add flour and mix well. Add stiffly beaten egg whites. Pour over the fruit in a buttered pan. Bake about 30 minutes at 300 degrees. This improves with age.

Fruit Cream Fudge

2 cups sugar
1 cup whipping cream
1 tablespoon butter
1 cup finely chopped dates, figs, prunes raisins, or nuts

Combine milk and cream and bring to a boil. Cook until syrup forms a soft ball when tested in cold water. Add butter and fruits or nuts. Take off the heat. Beat to a thick creamy consistency. Pour into a buttered pan.

Cherry Divinity Fudge

1 cup cherry juice from maraschino cherries
2 cups granulated sugar
1 cup corn syrup
2 egg whites
1 teaspoon cherry extract

Cook white sugar and water until crisp when dropped into cold water. Pour hot syrup mixture over stiffly beaten egg whites. Continue beating. Add flavoring. Pour into buttered pan.

Lemon Divinity Fudge

2 cup sugar
1 cup water
1 cup corn syrup
2 egg whites
1 teaspoon lemon extract
Zest of 1 lemon

Cook white sugar, syrup, and water until crisp in cold water. Pour hot syrup mixture over stiffly beaten egg whites. Continue beating until mixture losses its gloss. Add flavoring and zest. Pour into buttered pan.

Candied Orange Fudge

3 cups sugar
⅓ cup milk
½ cup water
2 teaspoons grated orange rind
¼ cup orange juice
¼ cup butter
¼ cup candied orange peel

Boil sugar, milk, and water for five minutes. Add orange rind, orange juice, and butter. Bring to the soft ball stage. Cool and beat until creamy then add orange peel that has been finely chopped. Pour into buttered dish and mark into squares when cooled enough.

Fig Fudge

¼ pound chopped figs
¼ teaspoon ground ginger
Butter the size of a walnut
2 cups sugar
1 cup cold water
Pinch of salt

Boil the ingredients together, stirring frequently for five or more minutes. Remove from heat and beat until the fudge begins to thicken and becomes creamy. Pour into a buttered dish and cool. Mark into squares.

Fresh Orange Fudge

1 tablespoon butter
2 cups sugar
¾ cup half and half or whipping cream
2 tablespoons grated orange rind
1 cup chopped pecans
¼ teaspoon cream of tartar
1 teaspoon lemon juice
6 tablespoons fresh orange juice

Melt butter and add orange rind. Add remaining ingredients except nuts and cook as you would any other fudge, to a soft ball stage. Remove from heat and allow to cool slightly. Add nuts and beat until smooth and creamy. Pour into buttered glass cake pan. When cold, candy may be rolled into balls and dipped into melted chocolate.

Cocoanut Fudge

1 envelope gelatin
¼ cup cold water
1 cup milk
2 cups sugar
½ tablespoon butter

¼ teaspoon salt
1 teaspoon vanilla
1 cup fresh shredded cocoanut

Bring sugar and milk to a boil and cook to the soft ball stage. Pour cold water in bowl and sprinkle the gelatin on top of water and soften gelatin. Add the gelatin to the hot candy mixture. Add butter, salt and vanilla as well. Beat until creamy. Add cocoanut and turn out into buttered flat pan.

Fresh and Fruity Fudge

2 squares chocolate
unsweetened
¾ cups sugar
Dash of salt
2 tablespoons butter
1 teaspoon vanilla
4 tablespoons candied
cherries

4 tablespoons candied
pineapple
4 tablespoons figs
4 tablespoons raisins
4 tablespoons blanched
pistachios

Add chocolate to milk and melt over low heat. Cook until
mixture is blended well. Stirring constantly, add sugar, and
salt. Dissolve sugar and bring mixture to a boil. Boil over low
heat to soft ball stage without stirring. Remove from the heat
adding butter and vanilla. Cool until warm to touch. Beat until
mixture becomes thick and creamy. Add fruits and nuts. Turn
into buttered pan. Top with additional nuts if you so desire.

Short Fruit Fudge

2 cups sugar
1 cup milk
2 tablespoons cocoa
2 tablespoons shortening
1 teaspoon vanilla

1 teaspoon lemon juice
½ cup chopped nuts
½ cup raisins
2 tablespoons cream
Pinch of salt

Put shortening, sugar, cocoa, salt, and milk into saucepan and
stir until it boils and forms a soft ball when tested in a cup of
cold water. Remove from fire and add raisins, cream, nuts,
extracts, and beat the mixture until thick and creamy. Put back
on fire and heat, stirring constantly until melted then pour into
oiled tins. When it is cooled, you can mark off the squares.

Tutti-Frutti Fudge

1 ⅓ cups milk
4 ounces chocolate
4 cups sugar
2 tablespoons white corn
syrup
½ teaspoon salt
¼ cup butter

4 teaspoons vanilla
⅓ cup each candied
cherries, pineapple and
raisins
Coconut or pecans optional
(see below)

Melt chocolate and butter over low heat. Stir in the sugar, syrup, and salt. Cook over a medium heat bringing the mixture to a boil. Stir constantly to a soft ball stage. Remove from heat and cool to lukewarm without stirring. Add the butter, cherries, raisins, pineapple, and vanilla. Beat until the mixture turns dull and pour it into a buttered pan. (Optional)When candy is cooled and can be handled, roll the fudge into balls then roll them in coconut or finely chopped nuts.

Raisin Fudge

2 cups sugar
1 cup milk
2 tablespoons cocoa
2 tablespoons shortening
1 teaspoon vanilla

½ cup chopped walnuts
½ cup raisins
2 tablespoons cream
Pinch of salt

Put shortening, sugar, cocoa, salt and milk into pan and stir until it boils and forms a soft ball when tested in cold water. Remove from fire add raisins, cream, nuts, and extracts. Beat mixture until thick and creamy. Pour mixture into cold candy tins or a buttered flat pan.

Fresh Cherry Fudge

2 ⅔ cups sugar
⅓ cup white syrup
1 cup light cream
3 heaping tablespoons cocoa
1 heaping tablespoon butter
2 teaspoons vanilla
2 cups fresh pitted cherries

Combine and stir well all ingredients. Cook on medium heat and avoid stirring while cooking until the thermometer reaches 232 to 234 degrees. Remove from fire and cool. Add butter and vanilla. Beat until creamy and add cherries. Pour up into buttered pan and allow to set up.

Fruity Fudge

2 ¼ cups sugar
1 cup evaporated milk
¾ cup butter
10 large marshmallows – sliced
6 ounces white chocolate - chopped

1 cup pecans
¼ cup candied cherries
¼ cup candied pineapple
½ teaspoon lemon flavoring
¼ teaspoon vanilla

Combine sugar, milk, and butter bring to a boil over medium heat, stirring until sugar is dissolved. Cook to soft ball stage. Remove from heat and add remaining ingredients. Beat until mixture begins to thicken and holds shape. Spread into shallow pan and allow to cool. Cut into squares.

Pineapple Fudge

1 cup evaporated milk
3 cups sugar
2 tablespoons butter
1 cup crushed pineapple
2 teaspoons lemon juice
½ cup pecan halves

Combine sugar, milk, and butter. Heat to boiling. Add
pineapple and cook to the soft ball stage. Do not let it burn or
scorch, takes about 25 minutes to reach this point. Cool. Add
lemon juice. Beat until it holds its shape. Pour into buttered pan
and mark in squares. Decorate with pecan halves.

Strawberry Fudge

2 cups sugar
½ cup water
½ cup light corn syrup
⅛ teaspoon salt
2 egg whites
½ teaspoon vanilla
Fresh strawberries chopped

Combine sugar, water, syrup, and salt and cook to 265 degrees.
Pour slowly over stiffly beaten egg whites. When stiff and it
has lost its gloss add the strawberries and pour into a greased
pan.

Avocado Fudge

1 ½ cup mashed avocados
½ teaspoon lemon flavoring
⅓ cup sweetened condensed milk
3 ½ cups sugar
½ cup water

Combine sugar, avocados, milk, and water. Cook to a soft ball stage. Remove from heat and add flavoring. Cool about 15 to 20 minutes. Beat until smooth. Pour into buttered pans to harden. Cut into squares.

Zucchini Fudge

1 ½ cup zucchini shredded
½ teaspoon lemon flavoring
½ cup sweetened condensed milk
3 ½ cups sugar
½ cup water
¼ cup cocoa

Cook zucchini, sugar, milk, and water to soft ball stage. Remove from heat, add flavoring and cocoa. Cool to room temperature. Beat until creamy. Pour into buttered pan 1 inch thick. Allow to firm up and cut into squares.

Blackberry Fudge

2 cups sugar
½ cup water
½ cup light corn syrup
⅛ teaspoon salt
2 egg whites
½ teaspoon vanilla
1 cup fresh blackberries

Combine sugar, water, syrup, and salt and cook to soft ball stage. Pour slowly over stiffly beaten egg whites. When it begins to get stiff and it has lost its gloss add the blackberries and pour into a greased pan.

Carrot Fudge

1 ½ cup carrots grated
½ teaspoon lemon flavoring
⅓ cup sweetened condensed milk
3 ½ cups sugar
½ cup water

Combine sugar, carrots, milk, and water. Cook to a soft ball stage. Remove from heat and add flavoring. Cool about 15 to 20 minutes. Beat until smooth. Pour into buttered pans to harden. Cut into squares.

Unexpected Parade

Freda Fiddlestick bedded down across the seats of her old faithful friend. Frankenstein might have died in the middle of the road, but it was still her home. The rundown vehicle was all she had left after that horrendous explosion in her house. She shook her head, recalling the chocolaty mess and the fire. Who knew fudge would start that big a fire?

"I sure thought that batch of fudge would work, too."

She fluffed her pillow and readied for bed. Officer Babs gave her a permit to stay at the curb overnight for one night only. What a nice woman Babs turned out to be. They were going to be friends; Freda could just feel it in her bones.

Sitting at her makeshift table, cold cream smeared all over her face, Freda took a quick inventory of her truck. Age was beginning to show on the old friend. They had been through many adventures together since that fateful night in July. That insurance man sure hadn't been very nice the next day. It was an accident with the stove.

If she was going to be doing this memory work, fudge was the answer. She stood at the stove she installed herself and put her ingredients in a pan. She looked around for her vanilla, but couldn't find it. Well, no problem. The adventurous woman reached for the special ingredients door. Pulling a dark bottle from the tiny cabinet, she added an ingredient no one would have thought of to the pan. She smiled and danced a couple of steps in place. This batch would be great. She poured the fudge into the flat pan. It had to set several hours before she could taste and see if it was as good as she hoped. Freda yawned and went off to bed.

The next morning she arose and quickly folded her bed away. For breakfast, she cut a large chunk of the secret ingredient fudge made the night before and poured herself a strong cup of coffee. There was nothing like strong coffee and fudge to wake a gal up from a restless night's sleep. She sipped the coffee, washing her palette of cotton balls. Swishing the brown liquid this way and that, she finally swallowed. She wrapped her lips around the square of fudge and bit into it. Savoring the luscious taste and texture, she allowed her mind to wander.

A knock on Frankenstein's front window startled her and she spilled coffee onto the fudge on her plate.

"Hmm, that should taste real good. Who's knocking at my door?"

"Officer Babs, ma'am. Miss Freda, I have to talk to you."

Freda opened the door and stepped outside. Most folks did not understand about hers and Frankenstein's arrangement. Anyway, she needed some fresh morning air. The fudge had been so good; she had to clear her mind before she could talk much anyway. Besides, the truck still reeked of her secret ingredient.

"What can I do you for this morning, Officer Babs?"

"I thought I better come and warn you. Joe and his friends will be here shortly. They'll help get your vehicle to a garage so it can be repaired."

Freda tapped her toe on the cement sidewalk. "Well, I really don't have the funds to fix old Frankenstein up right now. Is there some place we can park him until I get me a job and get some money together? Franky baby needs a makeover anyway."

"We have RV hookups at the city park. But this isn't an RV."

"Why sure Frankenstein is fixed up for an RV. I sleep in there all the time. Cook, too."

Babs looked at Freda as if she wondered about the woman's sanity. "Well, if you say you can live in this truck I suppose it would be all right. You will have to acquire a permit from city hall to stay at the RV Park. The boys can pull your vehicle to the park."

"Great. Hey did you ever hear of that group of rock and roll singers who had a hot tub in their truck back in the 70's?"

"Yes, but I thought that was just a hoax." Babs scratched her head.

"Well, I don't have a hot tub, but I do have a shower in there. I fixed old Frankenstein up real good one hot July. Even have him wired for electricity. Uh does your city park have facilities? Franky wasn't big enough for that."

"Of course."

"Great. How much longer until the boys get here? I sure did like that Joe. He has a tush on him anyone would love."

"It won't be but a few minutes. You're right about his tush. It is well rounded, but, he has a real cute girlfriend. I sort of like her, even though she is young enough to be his daughter. Here they come now."

"Great, I'll get things battened down inside. Can you handle hooking the truck up to the tow bar?"

"Of course I can, I've been doing stuff like that since I was a kid."

Once back inside the truck, Freda tied everything in place the same way she had done many times before. Her work went fast and smooth, leaving her a minute or two to change blouses. The shiny bling-bling blouse was a leftover from her disco days, one of only a few things saved before her house crumbled into ash, but she loved it and it slid easily over her ample figure. "This should do the trick." She preened in front of the small mirror only a moment. Quickly she turned to the cassette player and plugged in a tape. It would start to play as soon as they started moving. That was another trick she fixed up for her new business. Ice cream trucks had music, why not Frankenstein?

Emerging from the truck Freda delighted in the whistles and catcalls greeting her. She twirled and bowed. "Thank you. Thank you all."

Joe had Frankenstein's bumper hooked to the tow bar and Freda climbed into the back of his pickup.

"What are you doing now?" Officer Babs frowned.

"Well, I want to watch where we are going. If it is all right for me to ride back here."

"I suppose, just this once." Babs shook her head and got into the patrol car.

Slowly they drove down Main Street and headed towards the city park. Before they had rolled half a block,

24

Freda's cassette began to play the death march. The citizens of Sling Shot came out of their homes to see what was happening. Men working nearby stopped what they were doing to see the strange event. With Officer Babs in the lead, soon a slow moving funeral type procession wound through the streets of Sling Shot.

Men, women, and children dropped out of activities and followed the truck on foot and in their own vehicles. With a captive audience, more or less, Freda sang out loudly her rendition of an old ballad.

"As I walked out in the streets of Sling Shot, As I walked out in Sling Shot one day. I saw and old cowgirl all dressed in bight bling-bling. All wrapped in gold lamé."

On and on she sang as they turned into the park. Freda urged the crowd to sing with her. After they arrived at the park and stopped, she took her bows.

"Thank you. Thank you all for the great send off for Frankenstein. Now, I have a treat for all of you who came to pay your respects to my dearly departed truck." She passed out samples of her new batch of fudge, with its unexpected ingredient. She walked among the people and listened to their praise of her cooking. Freda smiled and mingled more, passing out seconds of the fudge. That batch was a hit and that secret ingredient really made the folks happy. Her plan worked great!

Honey Fudge

2 cups sugar
¾ cup milk
¼ cup heavy cream (whipping cream works well)
1 square chocolate
¼ cup honey
3 tablespoons butter
1 teaspoon vanilla
1 cup nuts

Boil sugar, milk, cream, and chocolate. About 5 minutes. Add honey and butter. Boil to the soft ball stage. Cool and beat until thick Add the vanilla and nuts. Pour into buttered pan.

Mexican Fudge

1 cup milk
3 cups sugar
1 cup pecans
1 teaspoon vanilla

Bring the milk and only two cups of the sugar to a boil. Cook at the boil for 15 minutes. Melt remaining sugar in a skillet and add to the first sugar mixture. Stir in the pecans and vanilla then beat until of pouring consistency. Pour in a buttered pan and let it stand for a while before cutting.

Little Darling Fudge

¾ cups honey
1 square chocolate
1 cup cream
½ cup milk
½ cup butter
1 teaspoon vanilla

Boil the milk, honey and grated chocolate until it comes to the soft ball stage. Add half the cream and boil again to soft ball. Add the remaining cream and butter and boil again to the soft ball stage. Add vanilla and pour into an oiled pan. When cool, form into balls and roll into chopped nuts.

Mexican Skillet Fudge

2 cups sugar
3 tablespoons butter
1 teaspoon cinnamon
½ teaspoon salt
1 cup heavy cream
½ cup mini marshmallows
1 ½ cup chocolate chips
⅔ cup chopped pecans
1 teaspoon vanilla

Mix sugar, butter, cinnamon, salt, and milk in electric skillet. Set it on 280 degrees. Bring to a boil. Stir constantly to the soft ball stage. Add remaining ingredients. Stir until melted. Blend until smooth. Pour into buttered pan. Cut into squares.

Sherry Fudge

1 small package chocolate chips
2 tablespoons butter
¼ cup cooking sherry
1 egg yolk
1 pound powdered sugar
1 cup chopped pecans
1 teaspoon vanilla (optional)

Combine chocolate chips, butter, and sherry. Cook until melted. Use a double boiler for this. Add yolk to sugar and pour chocolate over sugar mixture. Make sure it is all mixed well. If needed, a few more drops of sherry may be added. Stir in the nuts and vanilla (optional). Put into buttered pan and refrigerate.

Tennessee Sipping Fudge

1 small package chocolate chips
2 tablespoons butter
¼ cup Tennessee sipping whiskey (favorite brand)
1 egg yolk
1 pound powdered sugar
1 cup chopped pecans
1 teaspoon vanilla

Combine chocolate chips, butter, and whiskey. Cook until melted. Use a double boiler for this. Add yolk to sugar and pour chocolate over sugar mixture. Make sure it is all mixed well. If needed, a few more drops of whiskey may be added. Stir in the nuts and vanilla. Put into buttered pan and refrigerate.

Chocolate-Mint Fudge

4 cups sugar
Pinch of salt
1 can evaporated milk
2 bags of chocolate chips
1 jar marshmallow crème
½ teaspoon peppermint extract
2 cups pecan halves

Mix the sugar, salt, and milk. Cook for about 7-9 minutes. Remove from heat and pour over the chips, and marshmallow crème. Mix until well blended. Add peppermint extract and pecan halves. Pour into buttered pan and let it set. Cut into squares.

Butter-Rum Fudge

4 cups sugar
1 ⅔ cups milk
1 cup butter
12 ounces chocolate chips
2 cups marshmallow cream
1 teaspoon rum or rum flavoring
1 ½ cups pecans

Stir together the sugar, milk, and butter. Bring these to a boil and cook to the soft ball stage. Pour hot mixture over the chocolate chips, and marshmallow cream. Stir it all together until smooth. Add rum or rum flavoring and pecans. Pour into buttered pan.

Coffee Fudge

2 cups sugar
1 cup strong coffee
1 teaspoon heavy cream
1 cup chopped nuts

Combine the sugar, coffee and cream. Bring to a boil. Cook at boil for about 8 minutes or to the soft ball stage. Add nuts and beat candy until smooth and creamy. Pour into buttered dish.

Graham Cracker Fudge

2 cups sugar
2 squares chocolate
1 cup cream
1 pound small marshmallows
2 cups crushed graham crackers
1 cup nuts
2 tablespoons butter
1 teaspoon vanilla

Combine sugar, cream, and chocolate. Cook on medium until the mixture reaches the soft ball stage. Stir occasionally to keep from boiling over. Add marshmallows, graham crackers, nuts, butter, and vanilla. Mix until smooth and pour into a buttered pan.

Coconut Potato Fudge

¼ cup hot cooked mashed potatoes
1 teaspoon butter
2 ¼ cup powdered sugar
1 ½ cup coconut
½ teaspoon vanilla
Dash of salt
2 squares of unsweetened chocolate

Mix potatoes and butter. While beating, add sugar a little at a time. Stir in coconut, vanilla, and salt. Spread into buttered brownie pan and spread melted chocolate over potato mixture. Chill and serve.

Coconut Cream Fudge

2 cups sugar
1 cup whipping cream
1 tablespoon butter
1 cup coconut
1 teaspoon vanilla

Combine milk and cream and bring to a boil. Cook until syrup forms a soft ball when tested in cold water. Add butter, vanilla, and coconut. Take off the heat. Beat to a thick creamy consistency. Pour into a buttered pan.

Sour Cream Fudge

2 cups sugar
1 cup sour cream
Dash salt
1 teaspoon vanilla
2 tablespoons butter
1 cup chopped nuts

Cook sugar, cream, and salt over low heat. Stir occasionally to soft ball stage. Remove from heat add vanilla and butter. Cool and beat until the gloss is gone. Stir in pecans and pour into buttered pan.

Chocolate Sour Cream Fudge

3 cups sugar
1 cup sour cream
$\frac{1}{8}$ teaspoon soda
4 tablespoons dark corn syrup
6 tablespoons cocoa
$\frac{1}{8}$ teaspoon salt
1 teaspoon vanilla
1 cup chopped pecans

Combine everything except vanilla and pecans. Stir as little as possible and cook over medium heat to soft ball stage. Allow mixture to cool so that you can touch the bottom of the pan comfortably. Add vanilla and begin to beat at this point. When the glossy look is gone, add chopped pecans and pour into buttered pan.

White Sour Cream Fudge

2 cups sugar
2 tablespoons corn syrup
2 tablespoons butter
1 cup sour cream
1 teaspoon vanilla
1 cup walnuts

Thoroughly mix sugar, syrup, butter, and sour cream. If sour cream needs to be thinned, add enough milk to make it the consistency of thick whipping cream. Cook over low heat to soft ball stage. Cool and add vanilla and nuts. Beat until thick and holds its shape. Pour into buttered pan. Let cool and cut into squares.

Brown Sugar Sour Cream Fudge

3 cups brown sugar
1 cup sour cream
Pinch of salt
¼ cup butter
1 teaspoon vanilla
1 cup chopped walnuts

Combine sugar and cream and bring to a boil. Boil to soft ball stage. Remove from heat. Add butter and salt. Beat until mixture becomes a little grainy. Add vanilla and nuts and mix. Pour into buttered pan to cool.

Buttermilk Fudge

1 cup buttermilk
1 teaspoon soda
2 cups sugar
3 tablespoons white syrup
1 teaspoon vanilla
1 cup nuts

Mix the buttermilk and soda and let it stand for 5 minutes.
After 5 minutes, add the sugar and syrup and begin cooking
until the temperature reaches 238 degrees. Remove from heat
and cool to lukewarm. Add vanilla and nuts and beat until it
thickens and holds its shape. Pour into a buttered pan and cool.
Cut into squares after it has cooled.

Peanut Raisin Fudge

4 cups sugar
1 ½ cups milk
2 teaspoons corn syrup
1 cup chopped raisins
½ cup peanut butter
1 ½ teaspoon vanilla

Combine sugar, milk, and syrup in a saucepan and bring it to a
soft ball when dropped in cold water. Remove from heat and
add peanut butter, raisins, and vanilla. Let it stand until just
warm. Beat until creamy and smooth. Pour into well-buttered
pan and when cool you can cut it into squares.

Cream Cheese Fudge

1 small package cream cheese
2 cups powdered sugar
2 squares bitter chocolate
¼ teaspoon vanilla
⅓ teaspoon salt
¾ cup chopped nuts

Cream the cheese with the sugar then add melted chocolate.
Add vanilla, salt, and nuts mixing thoroughly. If the fudge
becomes too hard, add a teaspoon or so of cream when mixing
in the vanilla and nuts. Press into a buttered pan and cool in the
refrigerator for about 15 minutes

Jalapeno Fudge

1 cup butter
5 cups sugar
1 large can milk
3 packages chocolate chips
3 ounces marshmallow crème
¼ cup chopped jalapeno
2 teaspoons vanilla
1 cup chopped pecans
1 cup coconut

Mix butter, jalapeno, sugar, and milk. Boil hard for about 8
minutes. Add chips and stir until well blended. Add the
marshmallow cream and mix it up. Remove from the heat and
add vanilla, pecans, and coconut. Pour into greased pan and
cool before cutting into squares.

Chocolate Chili Fudge

3 cups sugar
3 heaping tablespoons
cocoa
¼ cup crystal white syrup
1 cup milk

1 tablespoon cayenne
pepper
½ stick butter
2 teaspoons vanilla
1 ½ cups nuts

Mix the sugar, cocoa, cayenne pepper, and salt before adding the syrup. Cook this mixture until it reaches the soft ball stage. It will form a soft lump when dropped into cold water. Remove from heat and add butter. When the butter is melted and the pot is cool to the touch, add vanilla and nuts beating until creamy. Pour into a buttered dish.

Cinnamon Coffee Fudge

1 cup chopped nuts
3 cups chocolate chips
1 can sweetened condensed milk
2 tablespoons strong coffee-cooled
1 teaspoon cinnamon
⅛ teaspoon salt
1 teaspoon vanilla

Put the nuts in a glass baking dish and microwave them for four minutes. Set aside for later.
In microwave bowl, mix chocolate chips, milk, coffee, cinnamon, and salt. Do not cover. Microwave for 1 ½ minutes. Stir until smooth. Add vanilla and nuts. Spread into a buttered pan and refrigerate covered for 2 hours.

Cinnamon Fudge

2 cups sugar
3-4 tablespoons cocoa
1 cup milk
2 tablespoons butter
Pinch of salt
1 teaspoon vanilla
1 tablespoon cinnamon

Cook everything except butter until soft ball stage. Add vanilla and butter. Cool without stirring. Beat until it loses its shine. Add nuts and pour into a buttered platter.

Explosion of Chocolate

KABOOM! Freda flew out the back door of the old truck and landed on her behind.

"Wow! What was that for?" She rubbed the object of her embarrassment and looked up at Frankenstein.

"Why did you eject me that way?"

Chocolate oozed from the back doors. It spread on the ground, inching toward her like evening's tide. Slowly she backed away. "HELP! It's like the Green Blob." Folks from the surrounding area rushed to see what Freda was cooking up this time.

"What happened?"

"Well, if I knew that I wouldn't have let it happen." Freda dusted her seat and watched the chocolate creep toward the street.

Sirens blasted through the still night air. Lights flashed brightly as Officer Babs drove her new patrol car through the park entrance. Pulling up next to the RV hookup, she jumped from the vehicle and ran to where Freda stood.

"What's going on here?"

"Who knows?" Freda shrugged, pointed to the truck and the molten chocolate as it continued to flow toward them. "I think I created a monster this time instead of fudge."

Everyone watched the syrupy mess edge closer and closer to the patrol car.

Freda grabbed a shovel from one of the men standing nearby and began shoveling dirt onto the chocolate blob. "I think you better call the fire department. I can't control this stuff."

"What is it?"

"It is supposed to be fudge, but I added another secret ingredient and was cooking it in the pressure cooker. I'm not sure, but I think I made chocolate blob, or blubber or something like that." Frantically, Freda shoveled a dam around the patrol car. She didn't want to be responsible for Officer Babs needing another new patrol car, like the last time.

"Well, we had better get the car out of the way. I do not want that hot stuff melting my tires. The mayor is already mad at me for wrecking the old one after eating some of your fudge the other day."

"Good, I'm getting tired of shoveling this dirt. Besides, I don't think my fudge was the reason you wrecked the car, was it?"

Babs shrugged, stepped back, and slid behind the wheel. Before she moved the vehicle, she leaned out the window and asked. "What did you put in that stuff anyway?"

Freda looked at Babs and smiled. "I can't tell you for fear it might incriminate me."

"Uh-huh, that's what I thought." Freda climbed into the patrol car.

"I think I have created a lake around us and I can't get out from the circle of fudge either. Can I ride it out with you?" Freda hoped on the hood of the car and held the shovel across her lap.

Babs nodded and tuned her microphone to the fire station. "Get the firemen down here to the park on the double. I have a mess of something for them to wash away. Uh-huh. Yes. They need their hoses and the water truck. No. I cannot control the oozing mess. No. It isn't a fire. Della Laverne, just call Joe. Get him and the men on the truck, and send them to the park. Yes. It is Miss Freda again."

Freda grinned. She had already become famous in the small town of Sling Shot. Everyone liked her despite the mishaps, and that was a good thing.

"The firemen are on their way." Babs gunned the patrol car out of the oozing chocolate, nearly losing Freda. She then parked away from the disaster site.

Freda slid off the hood, nodded, then leaned on the shovel. "That's good."

Within minutes, the firefighters were at the city park with their lights flashing and hoses ready.

"Where's the fire, Babs?" Joe stood before her in his bunker gear ready to fight whatever flame there was to fight.

"Not a fire, but I think we need to wash away all this chocolate goo trying to take over the park. Can you or one of the boys get into that truck and turn the heat off under that pressure cooker without getting anyone hurt?"

"Well, Babs, does a frog have hair?"

Freda could tell Babs loved the way he said things. She nearly melted at his off-color joke.

"Joe, you say the darnedest things."

Joe grinned, and slapped her on the back. "Babs, you are a good egg. We'll get this mess cleaned up in no time."

Freda sneaked up behind Babs and heard the woman sigh. "Confident little cuss isn't he?" She admired Joe as he walked away from them.

"Has a right to be. He's been fire chief for more than six years. Sling Shot residents sure do like the way he works. Keep electing him for some reason."

"Still got a girlfriend huh?

"Yep."

"Have they been together long?"

"Since high school."

"Yep. Ah-huh?"

Babs turned beet red.

"I see the way you look at him. We can do something about that if you want to. I mean heck, I been matchmaking practically all my life."

Bab's ears turned a darker shade of red.

"I don't know what you are talking about. I was telling you why he has a right to be confident. He posed for the fireman's poster and calendar one year. Sure wish I'd saved that calendar. I'd show it to you. He looked delicious in that picture. You know Freda; I might just take you up on that matchmaking business. Nah, his girl would be hurt too much if someone like me took him away from her. Better leave well enough alone."

Freda shook her head. She might drop it for now, but sooner or later, Joe would see what he was missing in Officer Babs. "Shoot, girlfriend, I don't need a calendar to show me why the women of this town keep electing him as fire chief. I bet he has a lot of calls to get cats out of trees, doesn't he?"

"As a matter of fact, he does."

Freda looked around and sure enough, mostly women gathered to witness the commotion. She never failed to use an opportunity to further her research. As the men on the fire

42

crew cleaned up the chocolate gooey mess, she went inside the truck and pulled out a couple of trays of fudge. The residents of Sling Shot bunched around her like a flock of geese on a worm. Each person took at least two samples from the trays.

Once the firefighters finished cleaning up the chocolate, they hovered around her for their reward, too. No one went away without a piece of fudge in his or her hand. Freda furnished enough fudge for all to have a taste. She listened to the comments about her explosive candy making techniques, but most of all she listened to the praise of her fudge.

Cooking the fudge was easy. Marketing however interested her the most. With the mishap of the pressure cooker, she had gathered a crowd and a mess turned out to be a good thing. She could just see the headlines, FIDDLESTICK AND FRANKENSTEIN COOK FUDGE. FIREMEN CLEAN UP CHOCOLATY MESS. Well, something like that would be good for her new business. She hadn't been in Sling Shot but about a week and already she had repeat customers. A business she would open as soon as she procured the money she needed.

Freda popped a nice square of chocolaty peanut butter fudge into her mouth. Not bad. Not bad at all.

Peanut Butter Fudge Roll

4 cups sugar
1 ⅔ cup evaporated milk
1 stick butter
4 tablespoons cocoa
Pinch of cream of tartar
1 cup peanut butter

In a sauce pan, bring to boil, the sugar, milk, butter, cocoa, and cream of tartar. Boil it on low until it forms a soft ball in water. Cool for 15 minutes. Beat it until it loses its shine and begins to thicken. Pour it out onto waxed paper and start working it. When it is thick enough to spread the peanut butter on it, spread the peanut butter on the flattened candy and roll it up. You will have to work quickly so it does not harden too much before you have it rolled. The wax paper will help you roll the candy. Chill and slice.

White Peanut Butter Fudge

3 cups sugar
1 cup milk
1 stick butter

½ teaspoon salt
1 teaspoon vanilla
3 tablespoons peanut butter

Cook the sugar, milk, butter, and salt until the soft ball stage is reached. Remove from the burner then add vanilla and peanut butter. Beat the mixture until it becomes thickened. Pour into a buttered pan to cool before serving.

Peanut Butter-Oatmeal Fudge

5 tablespoons cocoa
2 ¾ cups sugar
½ cup butter
½ cup milk
½ cup peanut butter
3 cups old fashioned oatmeal
1 teaspoon vanilla

For two minutes, boil the cocoa, sugar, butter, and milk.
Remove from heat adding peanut butter, oats, and vanilla. Mix
it all together and pour it into a buttered dish. Cool and cut it
into squares.

Peanut Butter Banana Fudge

1 ½ cups mashed bananas
1 cup dark brown sugar
1 cup sugar
½ cup peanut butter
1 cup half and half
Pinch of salt

Combine all ingredients and cook until it reaches the soft ball
stage. Cool and pour into buttered pan.

Peanut Butter Brown Sugar Fudge

1 cup dark brown sugar
1 cup sugar
½ cup peanut butter
1 cup half and half
Pinch of salt

Combine all ingredients in a sauce pan. Cook until it reaches the soft ball stage. Pour into buttered pan to cool.

Cold Peanut Butter Fudge

2 squares chocolate
2 tablespoons butter
2 tablespoons peanut butter, creamy
1 teaspoon vanilla
2 cups powdered sugar
4-5 tablespoons milk

Melt chocolate and butter. Stir in peanut butter and vanilla until smooth. Gradually add the sugar alternating with the milk. This makes a stiff candy, Do not try to soften, it will ruin it. Press the fudge into a pan and cut into squares.

Million Dollar Peanut Butter Pecan Fudge

4 ½ cups sugar
1 can milk
⅓ cube butter
16 ounces peanut butter chips
1 pound chocolate bar
1 jar marshmallow crème
2 cups pecans

Boil the sugar, butter, and milk for five minutes. Pour the hot mixture over the chips, chocolate bar, and marshmallow crème. Stir until it is smooth and creamy. Pour into well-buttered pan and score for cutting into squares later.

Granny's Peanut Butter Fudge

2 cups sugar
½ cup white syrup
½ cup water
Pinch salt
2 tablespoons peanut butter

Boil the first four ingredients until it makes a soft ball when dropped in cold water. Add peanut butter and let it cool slightly before you stir it then beat it until it begins to thicken. Pour it in a buttered pan.

Peanut Butter Walnut Fudge

2 cups sugar
4 heaping tablespoons peanut butter
1 teaspoon vanilla
½ cup milk
½ cup corn syrup
1 cup walnuts

Mix sugar, milk, and syrup. Bring it all to a boil. Test it in cold water to see if it will form a soft ball. Take it off the burner then add the vanilla and peanut butter. Beat it with an electric mixer until it is no longer glossy. Add nuts and pour into buttered pan.

Chocolate Peanut Butter Fudge

2 cups sugar
⅔ cups milk
4 tablespoons cocoa
½ cup peanut butter
¼ cup butter
1 teaspoon vanilla

Combine sugar, milk, and cocoa then cook on medium high heat until it boils and reaches the soft ball stage. Remove from heat then add the peanut butter, butter and vanilla without stirring. Allow to cool for about 15 minutes. Stir to combine the added ingredients. Cool and cut into squares.

Peanut Fudge

2 cups brown sugar
1 cup milk
2 tablespoons shortening
14 teaspoon salt
1 cup chopped peanuts
1 teaspoon vanilla

Boil milk, sugar, shortening, and salt until it forms a soft ball.
Remove from heat then add nuts and vanilla. Beat until
creamy and pour into buttered pan.

Peanut Butter Cocoa Fudge

1 cup + 3 tablespoons creamy peanut butter
1 cup butter
3 ½ cups powdered sugar
3 tablespoons cocoa
1 tablespoon vanilla

Heat the butter and peanut butter together over medium heat.
Remove from fire and stir in powdered sugar, cocoa, and
vanilla. Pour this into a buttered pan and freeze for 30 minutes.

Chocolate Peanut Butter Fudge Too

1 egg well beaten
1 cup sugar
¾ cup cornstarch
⅓ cup milk
1 stick butter
2 tablespoons peanut butter
2 tablespoons chocolate extract
1 pound box powdered sugar
½ cup nuts

Beat the egg and set aside. Blend sugar, and cornstarch. Add milk and bring to a boil stirring constantly. Boil the milk and sugar mixture for 5 minutes. Remove from heat. Whip a small amount of the hot mixture into the egg to temper it. Slowly pour the egg mixture into the milk and sugar mixture stirring constantly. Boil for 2 minutes. Remove from heat and stir in the butter, peanut butter, and extract. When this becomes smooth return to heat until mixture becomes thickened. Pour hot mixture into bowl and add powdered sugar and beat until it is smooth then add the nuts and beat until mixture becomes stiff. Press this into a buttered pan and cool before eating.

Peanut Butter Fudge

1 cup sugar
2 tablespoons butter
1 teaspoon vanilla
¼ pound peanut butter
1 cup brown sugar
½ cup evaporated milk
1 cup marshmallows
Pinch of salt

Cook sugar, salt, butter, and milk to a soft ball stage. Add marshmallows and peanut butter just before removing from heat. Add flavoring. Beat until mixture is creamy and thick. It will hold its shape when it is ready. Drop it from a teaspoon to test its readiness. Pour into a well-buttered shallow pan. Let set and cut into squares.

Papa's Peanut Butter Fudge

2 cups sugar
1 cup evaporated milk
1 cup crunchy peanut butter
7 ounce jar marshmallow cream

2 tablespoons butter
1 teaspoon vanilla
Pecans

Bring the sugar and milk to a boil. Add the peanut butter, marshmallow cream, butter, and vanilla. Bring this mixture to the soft ball stage then take off the heat. Beat until creamy and add pecans. Pour into buttered pan. Cool and cut in squares.

Mama's Peanut Butter Fudge

2 cups sugar
1 cup milk
1 jar marshmallow cream
1 12-ounce jar peanut butter
1 teaspoon vanilla

Mix sugar and milk. Cook to the soft ball stage. Remove from heat. Stir in marshmallow cream and peanut butter. Add vanilla beating until creamy. Pour into buttered pan to cool

Good Peanut Butter Fudge

2 cups sugar
⅔ cups milk
1 pint marshmallow cream
1 cup chunky peanut butter
1 tablespoon butter
1 teaspoon vanilla
Peanuts

Bring to a boil, sugar and milk. Boil to soft ball stage. Put remaining ingredients into warm mixing bowl and add the hot sugar mixture. Beat until mixed well. Pour into a buttered pan and let set overnight.

Better Peanut Butter Fudge

1 pound light brown sugar
1 tablespoon butter
3 tablespoons granulated sugar
½ cup milk
1 teaspoon cornstarch
1 teaspoon vanilla
1 jar smooth peanut butter (8 ounces)

Mix brown sugar, butter, granulated sugar, and milk. Dissolve
the sugars and cook until the mixture forms a soft ball in cold
water. Add cornstarch dissolved in a small amount of cold
water. Take off heat immediately and beat until cooled. Add
vanilla and peanut butter. Pour into buttered flat cake pan and
allow to set up before cutting into squares.

G. Vanoil

High School Fantasy Prom

"Fantasy. What better way to build a fantasy world than to use candy? Better yet, how about making a fantasy land castle and everything that goes with it, out of fudge?" Freda Fiddlestick questioned the new parent sponsor sitting at the patio table.

"This year's Winter Senior Prom theme is fantasy. I don't really care what kind of fantasy." Robyn Etta Gandy, head of the committee threw up her hands. "Well, you know there can't be anything involving sex in the fantasy land. I told each senior student to develop a fantasy theme. These are the themes they submitted. I am not thrilled with most of them. You can imagine what some of those boys want to do with the fantasy theme. We just are not going there. The committee judged the suggestions and I have five to choose from, and I don't want to be the one to choose." Robyn Etta paced around the table, ranting about the fantasies of the senior boys. "Since you have started working at the school, Miss Fiddlestick, we thought you could help us select a theme."

"I'm not sure I can judge which is the best, but I'll give it a shot. I can only tell you which one I like best." She tapped her fingers on the table. "I want to help do the work, too. I just love being involved with any type of fantasy. Besides, I like those kids. They're pretty special people. Many a night they have come over here to the park and entertained me. They keep me young just listening to their complaints and such."

Ms. Gandy rolled her eyes and muttered. "Good kids, indeed. You didn't read their ideas of a fantasy prom."

Freda Fiddlestick leaned her chair back against Frankenstein and chuckled while she read the five themes presented. "Some of the boys must have written these just to shock you, deary."

"Well, they certainly got what they wanted, if that was the case." Robyn Etta sighed.

"This is a great suggestion." Freda tossed one of the papers on the table. "I choose these two. It's a toss-up between them. Which do you like the best?" Another paper floated to the tabletop in beat with the music on the radio.

Robyn Etta picked up the two entries. She sat with her head in her hands. "I don't care which one of these; let's just do the 'eeney-meeney-miney-moe' thing. Frankly, I like your idea of a chocolate fantasy prom better than either of these." Robyn Etta shook her head.

"Suits me." Freda studied the harried woman for a few minutes. "Just the one I would have chosen. Now, all we have to do is get to work on it. Where are the builders for the base?" Freda Fiddlestick never allowed an opportunity to dance get away and this was no exception, she twirled and twisted and stomped her feet to a fast paced song on the radio. "This is going to be the greatest Senior Prom Sling Shot ever witnessed." Freda spied the police cruiser as it turned down the park road.

"Officer Babs," Freda motioned for her to pull the car into the park. "You're out cruising early tonight. Want to join us? We are about to embark on an adventure into the chocolate fantasy land of Sling Shot. Ms. Gandy and I have just settled on a theme for the Senior Prom and we're about to get to work. How about helping us?"

"I might as well. There's nothing going on in Sling Shot that needs my services anyway. What do you need?"

Freda grinned, and busted out laughing. "A plan. We are going to build a chocolate fantasy world for those kids. It is our duty to come up with a way to do it. I only know we will use chocolate and other fudges to build this fantasyland, but that is all I know." Freda felt her feet beginning to pick up the beat from the blasting radio again.

"Be careful, Freda. I don't what people thinking you are a loony tune dancing around this park in the middle of the day and such."

"I'll just tell them to come and talk to you, Babs. Everyone knows you're a straight shooter. With you as my friend, I don't figure I need to worry what others think. Tell me what you think about the fantasy thing." For hours they talked about the fantasyland, developing a plan of action.

The next day, the ladies set the senior class to work. Several weeks passed. The shop class helped build the base for the fantasy castle and clouds. Freda and Ms. Gandy worked in the school cafeteria to make the fudge needed for the construction of the scenery.

Once the construction crew finished building the props, Freda knew how much more fudge she needed to cook. With the candy set and hardened a little extra, it was time to get the castle bricked. The students and their sponsors went to work stacking fudge bricks against the wooden framework.

The principal, Mrs. Sammy J. Burkelheimer, even got in on the action. She gave them permission to turn the thermostat down low to keep the candy from melting and she helped carry the large pans of fudge to the construction site.

They built a dark chocolate fudge castle on a cloud of fluffy white divinity, smothered in white chocolate fudge. The castle towered eleven feet tall by the time they finished. The students built an entire fantasy world complete with fudgy gargoyle sculptures to guard the serving tables.

Some of the school kitchen staff members helped make a table full of fudgy desserts and treats for the prom attendees. They dipped strawberries in fudge, made zucchini fudge cakes, and fudge covered meatballs. The tables were set with gold chargers and gold plated flatware. The gold trimmed chocolate goblets set the mood for a far out fantasy. A table at the entrance displayed roses for each girl, handmade from white chocolate fudge dyed red. Freda, Ms. Gandy, and Officer Babs stood in the doorway to review the miracle of fudge.

"Now, I call this a fantasyland." Freda clapped her hands together and twirled around a couple of times.

"For sure," Officer Babs sighed.

"Shall we all go home and get ready for the prom?" Freda could hardly wait to try on her new dress. "I have fashioned myself a dress for the prom. I'll bring the remainder of the fudge with me tonight. We have roses for the girls, so I have a special treat for the boys. They'll be thrilled." She locked the door behind her, giggled, and walked away.

"I hope no one turns the heat up in there before the prom is over." Babs smiled.

"I hope everyone brings a jacket to wear over their dresses." Ms. Gandy nodded at the maintenance man. "Good evening, Mr. Andrews."

Hours later, several people stood outside the auditorium waiting for someone to unlock the door. Freda had kept the key so no one could get in until she made her appearance. Minutes ticked off the clock and the students became restless. Just before time for the prom to start, she walked through the front door. Her gold lamé dress shone brightly under the florescent lights just the way she knew it would. She watched herself in the plate glass cases that held the school trophies. Taking a few fancy dance steps, she walked toward the auditorium door. She winked at Officer Babs and Ms. Gandy.

"This is a surprise for the boys." She held a large tray of foil-covered goodies high above her head.

"Here, Tommy, hold this. Don't peep inside though. I think you boys are going to love this batch of fudge. Once she unlocked the door, she took the fudge from Tommy and stepped inside the auditorium. Her feet hit something slippery, and her backside hit the floor. She slid down toward the front of the room holding the tray high in the air.

A heat wave in the room had melted everything. The castle resembled the leaning tower in Italy with streaks of brown peanut butter fudge running down its side. The cone shaped top had melted into a flat roof. The white chocolate oozed off the clouds and became an ocean of sticky candy instead. The roses on the tables wilted into dripping candle shapes.

Freda recovered from the fall and got to her feet. She hefted the tray of fudge and set it on the table.

"Well, this is a big mess. Someone must have turned the thermostat back up after we left." She fanned her flushed face. "No problem. We'll still have our fantasy prom. It's a cinch we can't dance on this chocolate covered floor. Ms. Gandy can you open the cafeteria door?"

She nodded.

"Officer Babs, put a sign on the front door for the others to trek on down to the cafeteria. One thing about chocolate, when it gets cold enough we can chip it off the floor. Ms. Gandy, will you get that thermostat back down to zero? It'll be much easier to clean up. Now, everything is all settled. You guys and dolls, listen up. You have the best opportunity to make your own fantasies come true, well, within reason of course." She chuckled at the looks of defeat on some of the boys' faces. "Only you can do it. I know all your hard work went kablooy." She spread her arms to the sky to indicate an explosion. "I've had this happen to me many times, but you're still here and we still have the food in the cold storage. When the D.J. arrives, then your night will be better. However, right now, let's dance on down to the cafeteria and get the party started."

"What about your dress?" Officer Babs, dressed in her uniform stepped away from the dripping garment.

Freda looked at her new dress and laughed. "Oh well, chocolate is expensive and so is gold. I'll just stand in the deep freeze for a few minutes and get this stuff right off my dress. I'll be good as new and the sweetest girl at the prom."

Freda led the prom members down the hall, chocolate dripping from her gold lame`. After she started some music, she stripped the foil from the racecar shaped chocolate fudge she brought for the guys and passed them out to each boy. "Now since the girls' roses wilted so to speak, you boys must share with your counterparts."

"Freda, you're the best. These fudge fastbacks are great." The boys fell back into their childhood playing with their treats. Freda made each fella the car of their dreams from fudge that afternoon with her special ingredient inside, champagne and cherries.

"I call this my sippin' fudge. You use a toothpick, puncture the tire, and sip out the liquid before you bite into the fudge.

The food for the prom was set on a table for the students to help themselves. The students laughed and danced. Even the chaperones had a nice time, especially those eating Freda's fudge.

Fantasy Fudge

3 cups sugar
¾ cup margarine
⅔ cup evaporated milk
1 - 12 ounce package semi-sweet chocolate chips
1 – 7 ounce jar marshmallow cream
1 cup chopped nuts
1 teaspoon vanilla

In a heavy saucepan, 2 ½ quart size, bring to a full rolling boil, sugar, margarine, and milk. Stir constantly. Boil for 5 minutes until mixture forms a soft ball when dropped in a cup of cold water. Be careful not to scorch the mixture. Dump in the chocolate chips stirring until melted. Add marshmallow cream and stir until melted. Add nuts and vanilla. Beat until smooth, and pour into a greased 13 X 9 inch pan. Cool and cut into squares.

White Maple Coconut Fudge

1 cup maple sugar
1 cup brown sugar
2 tablespoons butter
¼ cup maple syrup

¾ cup cream
½ cup shredded coconut
½ cup pecans

Put everything except coconut and nuts in a pan to boil. Cook to soft ball stage. Remove from burner. Add coconut and pecans. Beat until creamy. Pour into pan and sprinkle more nuts on top.

White Coconut Fudge

2 cups sugar
1 ½ cups milk
4 tablespoons corn syrup
¼ teaspoon salt
3 teaspoons butter
½ cup coconut
½ teaspoon vanilla
½ teaspoon coconut extract

Bring to a boil the sugar, milk, syrup, and salt. Cook to 235 degrees. Stir often. Remove from heat. Mix in butter and cool. Add coconut and extracts. Beat with spoon until mixture loses its gloss and pour into buttered pan for cooling.

Caramel Divinity Fudge

1 cup sugar
1 cup water
1 cup brown sugar
1 cup corn syrup
2 egg whites
1 teaspoon vanilla

Cook white sugar and caramelize before adding to water. Cook until crisp in cold water. In a separate pan at the same time, cook brown sugar and syrup until also crisp. Pour hot white syrup mixture over stiffly beaten egg whites. Continue beating and pour the brown sugar mixture over the egg whites as well. Add flavoring. Pour into buttered pan.

Divinity Fudge

1 cup sugar
1 cup water
1 cup brown sugar

1 cup corn syrup
2 egg whites
1 teaspoon vanilla

Cook white sugar and water until crisp in cold water. In separate pan at the same time, cook brown sugar and syrup until also crisp. Pour hot white syrup mixture over stiffly beaten egg whites. Continue beating and pour the brown sugar mixture over the egg whites as well. Add flavoring. Pour into buttered pan.

Golden Fudge

3 cups sugar
1 cup light corn syrup
3 tablespoons margarine
½ teaspoon salt
1 cup evaporated milk

½ cup water
2 teaspoons vanilla
1 cup chopped pecans

Combine sugar, syrup, margarine, salt, milk, and water in heavy saucepan. Stirring constantly, bring it to a boil. Cook quickly, stirring several times until it reaches the soft ball stage. Can be tested by dropping a small amount of sugar mixture into cold water. Remove from heat. Add vanilla and do not stir. Cool until lukewarm. Add pecans and beat until it becomes thickened and it loses its gloss. Drop in small mounds on waxed paper or spread in buttered pan.

White Fudge

2¼ cups sugar
½ cup sour cream
¼ cup milk
2 tablespoons butter
1 tablespoon light corn
syrup

¼ teaspoon salt
1 cup chopped walnuts or
pecans
½ cup quartered, candied
cherries

Combine sugar, cream, milk, butter, syrup and salt in a 2-quart saucepan. Stir over medium heat until the sugar mixture reaches a boil. Boil 9 to 10 minutes or to soft boil stage. Remove from heat and allow to stand about 1 hour. Add vanilla and beat until mixture just begins to lose its shine and holds its shape. Stir in walnuts and cherries, turn into buttered pan. Cool until firm before cutting.

Million Dollar Butterscotch Fudge

4½ cups sugar
½ teaspoon salt
1 can milk
2 tablespoons butter

12 ounces butterscotch
chips
1 pound white almond bark
1 jar marshmallow crème
2 cups pecans

Boil the sugar, butter and milk for five minutes. Pour the hot mixture over the chips, almond bark, and marshmallow crème. Stir until smooth and creamy. Pour into well-buttered pan and score for cutting into squares later.

Buttermilk Praline Fudge

3 cups sugar
1 ½ cups buttermilk
1 ½ teaspoons soda
1 ½ teaspoons vanilla
2 cups pecans

Bring the sugar, buttermilk and soda to a boil in a heavy kettle.
Stirring constantly over low heat, bring it up to the soft ball
stage. Remove from heat and add vanilla and pecans. Stir with
a wooden spoon until the mixture begins to thicken. Pour onto
a sheet cake pan that has been well buttered. This is better
eaten very thin.

Calico Fudge

1 ½ cups sugar
¾ cup brown sugar
⅔ cup milk
2 tablespoons butter
2 tablespoons light corn syrup
4 tablespoons peanut butter
6 large marshmallows- -cut into small pieces

Cook the milk, sugar, and syrup to the soft ball stage. Add the
butter and the peanut butter to the hot mixture, beating until it
is smooth and creamy. Pour over the marshmallows and pour
into a buttered pan.

Burnt Sugar Fudge

6 cups sugar

2 cups cream

¼ teaspoon soda

½ cup butter

1 tablespoon vanilla

3 cups chopped nuts

Mix 4 cups of the sugar add the cream in a heavy sauce pan. Bring it to a boil. Place the 2 cups of sugar into heavy skillet and place on heat to melt while stirring. Sugar must be all melted to look like brown sugar syrup. Don't burn it, keep the color light brown. Pour the melted sugar into the cream mixture. Mix well. Cook until the mixture makes a firm solid ball when dropped into cold water just before hard ball stage. Set off the fire and add the soda, stirring until the mixture foams up. Add butter and stir until melted. Allow to cool for 20 minutes before adding vanilla. Beat mixture until dull and heavy. Stir in nuts and pour into buttered pan. When it is cool, cut into squares.

Caramel Fudge

2 cups sugar

1 cup milk

2 tablespoons butter

 Pinch of salt

1 teaspoon vanilla

Melt the sugar to give it that caramel color, being careful not to burn it. Add to milk, salt, and butter that are already boiling. Boil to soft ball stage, cool and beat until no longer shiny. Pour into pan.

G. Vancil

Fudge Wrestlers in Sling Shot

Several women sat around a picnic table next to Frankenstein. Miss Avi Nell's pretended to be a radio announcer, her lifelong dream job. "Yes, folks, the headlines were not a misprint. This past week our sports fans brought in professional mud wrestlers for entertainment—not your garden variety wrestlers seen on television, but real live, bikini-clad mud wrestlers."

The women laughed at their friend's pretense.

"Mayor Roo-Roo said she had never seen such a display as the one she witnessed in the city park on Tuesday night. It seems a few of the men in Sling Shot put their heads together and decided the best summer sports event would be mud wrestling. The men pooled their money and obtained a pit for the girls to squirm around in. One got the brilliant idea to buy the largest cattle watering trough the local supply store stocked, build a fence and a platform to surround it." Avi Nell's took a deep breath before she started up again.

"When the Sling Shot wives discovered what type of wrestling and wrestlers were coming to town, they vowed to put a stop to the whole thing. Officer Babs kept the women in check so they didn't do anything illegal. The women gathered at the city park where Frankenstein and Miss Freda resided."

Freda stood up and took a twirling bow before her friends.

"They discussed a plan over coffee and fudge. Naturally. Miss Freda furnished the coffee, the fudge, and a plan."

The women giggled and grabbed another bite of fudge. Avi Nell's passed the pretend microphone to Freda.

"It was clear those women were too steamed up to think rationally. Therefore, I took over, since I am unattached, and told them there was a better way than to brand their men with hot pokers. Besides, that would only make more hot fannies in the mud."

The group of women roared with laughter.

Flower Pans took the microphone, and in her best teacher's voice announced further news. "The women moved the platform and the galvanized water trough under dark of night, and transferred it to the pavilion at the park. There was no way they would allow the men to fill this with mud, especially on the gym floor. They said the women's auxiliary had paid too much money for the gym floor to be ruined. Especially not by a bunch of near naked women who call themselves mud wrestlers. Miss Freda told her friends she would take care of filling the pit so there was no need in them staying away from home all night. Besides, they needed to get more details on the event and the husbands need not become suspicious.

The next day, the men went to fill the pit with dirt and water, they found it gone and naturally reported it to the police. Officer Babs explained to them she had moved the water trough so as not to ruin the gym floor. She further explained that having the wrestling event in the park would be better for their ticket box as they might entice passersby to the event. The men, gung-ho about this new turn of events, thanked her for her help and left."

The audience of women consumed another pan of fudge and a pot of coffee between guffaws at the different announcers. Flower Pans continued with her fake radio show.

"Meanwhile, the women, led by Miss Freda Fiddlestick filled the pit with sugar, milk, cocoa and other fudge making ingredients. The mass of ingredients somewhat resembled mud in the beginning, up until it began to set up and hardened."

Diva Devine shook her long black hair loose from its usual clip, and took over the microphone. "Unaware of their wives and girlfriends' plan, the men continued preparing a concession stand and other necessities for the event. It was only when the wrestling girls didn't show up on time that the men began to worry. What if their wives and girlfriends had stopped the wrestlers from coming into town?" Diva Devine swooshed her beautiful black hair over her shoulder.

"This, of course, was not the case. The women wrestlers were having a coffee and fudge break at the park with

71

Miss Freda and Officer Babs. Just like we are doing right this minute. Unbeknownst to the wrestlers, the other women of Sling Shot were putting the last phase of Miss Freda's plan into action. They took the wrestlers' bikinis and robes from their vehicle and went home to change. Once in the outfits, they all met back at Frankenstein's back door. The wrestler women were sound asleep because of a special ingredient in Miss Freda's fudge, one she usually saved for only herself."

The women in the park cheered at their cleverness. Miss Freda stood up, twirled, and spun around in the excitement the women created before she made a low curtsy.

Gwenella Rose, petite with gorgeous salt and pepper hair flipped on one side, took her turn being the announcer. She acted out the scenes as she talked. "The ladies of Sling Shot pulled the robes up close to their bodies and fashioned masks for their faces. The bell rang for the wrestling to begin, and Miss Freda, dressed in a creation of her own, a sequined bathing costume of the 1800s, announced that the lady wrestlers wanted to start the first round with the men in the pit. They needed the competition and invited the men to step into the hardening fudge wearing nothing but their boxers." Gwenella Rose giggled so hard she had to stop and catch her breath.

"Eagerly, the men stripped to their boxers, and stepped into the fudge. Miss Freda announced the match was about to begin. That's when everything hit the fan. Sling Shot's women, standing on the platform stripped off their robes. The men, stuck in the fudge tried to run, but there was no moving for them." Gwenella Rose passed the make-believe microphone to Della Laverne.

"Miss Freda informed the men, they should feel lucky only having to be stuck in fudge. The women of Sling Shot had wanted to put tar and feathers or cement in the pit, but she talked them out of such drastic measures. Another option the women suggested was to acquire a cattle prod or even branding irons to brand their men."

The women at the table went wild with each suggestion. Della Laverne held her hand up for silence. "Our Miss Freda talked the ladies out of all this and offered to make the men some coffee to wash down the fudge they were going to have to eat to get out. The men hung their heads in shame. Bringing women mud wrestlers to Sling Shot had been their worst idea yet. They declined the coffee, thanked Miss Freda for her courtesy, and her quick thinking. Miss Freda presented each man a small plastic spoon and told them to dig themselves out of the hole they had dug for themselves." Della Laverne held the make-believe microphone to Freda. "Do you have a comment, Miss Freda?"

"No comment."

The women laughed and ate more fudge.

"The women of Sling Shot sent the mud wrestlers packing, with a police escort. Officer Babs blasted on her siren all the way to the city limit sign. The men have sworn there will never again be mud wrestlers in Sling Shot, but fudge and Miss Freda are here to stay." Della Laverne finished her announcing with a low bow.

The women around Miss Freda's table cheered loudly. The birds roosting in the trees fluttered in unison making the women's applause even louder.

Miss Freda picked up the spoon they used for a microphone and made an announcement. "I am here to stay! I bought a house, and will be moving in this next week. Ladies have some more fudge. I understand that dark chocolate is good for you these days."

Best Chocolate Fudge

3 cups sugar
1 cup cream
4 tablespoons cocoa
1 tablespoon light corn syrup
1 tablespoon butter
1 teaspoon vanilla

Place sugar, cream, cocoa, and corn syrup into a saucepan. Stir until mixed well. Bring to a boil over low heat without stirring until it makes a soft ball when tested in water. Remove from heat and add butter. Stir for a while and add vanilla. Pour into a buttered pan. When cooled cut into squares.

Dark Chocolate Foolproof Fudge

3 cups semi-sweet chocolate chips
1 can sweetened condensed milk
Dash salt
1 cup pecans
1 ½ teaspoons vanilla

In a microwave safe glass bowl preferably with handle, mix milk, chocolate chips, and salt. Cook mixture for 3 minutes on full power, or until the chips are melted. Stir after each 1 ½ minutes of cooking. Stir in remaining ingredients and pour into a foil lined pan. Cool and remove the fudge from the pan to be cut into squares.

Chocolate Fudge

3 cups sugar
3 squares chocolate
1 ⅓ cups milk
⅛ teaspoon salt
3 tablespoons butter
1 teaspoon vanilla
⅔ cups nuts

Mix sugar, chocolate, milk, salt, and butter. Boil gently, stirring frequently until soft ball forms when portion is tested in cup of cold water. Set aside 20 minutes, add vanilla. Beat until thick and creamy. Add nuts and pour onto buttered pan. Cut in squares when cold.

Old Fashioned Chocolate Fudge

2 pounds brown sugar
1 cup milk
2 tablespoons butter
2 teaspoons vanilla
1 cup nuts
2 squares chocolate

Let the sugar and milk cook together, stirring until sugar is dissolved. Add melted chocolate and let it boil to the soft ball stage. Remove from fire and add vanilla, butter, and nuts. Beat vigorously by hand for 5 minutes using a wooden spoon. Turn into a buttered pan and mark into squares.

Old Fashioned Fudge

3 cups sugar
¼ cup corn syrup
3 squares chocolate
¼ teaspoon salt
1 cup canned milk
¾ cups pecans

Bring all ingredients except nuts to a boil and cook until it reaches the soft ball stage. Cool until lukewarm to the touch. Beat until creamy and thickening starts. Add the nuts and spread in the buttered pan.

Chocolate Divinity Fudge

1 cup sugar
1 cup water
1 cup brown sugar
1 cup corn syrup
2 squares chocolate
2 egg whites
1 teaspoon vanilla

Cook white sugar and water until crisp in cold water. In separate pan at the same time, cook brown sugar, chocolate squares and syrup until also crisp. Pour hot white syrup mixture over stiffly beaten egg whites. Continue beating and pour the brown sugar mixture over the egg whites as well. Add flavoring. Pour into buttered pan.

Cream Fudge

2 cups sugar
1 cup whipping cream
1 tablespoon butter

Combine milk and cream and bring to a boil. Cook until syrup forms a soft ball when tested in cold water. Add butter and take off the heat. Beat until thick and creamy. Pour into a buttered pan.

Chocolate Cream Fudge

2 cups sugar
1 cup whipping cream
1 tablespoon butter
2 squares bitter chocolate chipped up

Combine milk and cream, and bring to a boil. Cook until syrup forms a soft ball when tested in cold water. Add butter and chocolate. Take off the heat. Beat to a thick creamy consistency. Pour into a buttered pan.

A Coconut Fudge

2 tablespoons milk
1 tablespoon corn syrup
½ stick butter
1 teaspoon vanilla
Dash of salt
1 package Magic Frosting sugar
1 ½ cups flaked coconut
2 squares chocolate semi-sweet

In a double boiler, mix milk, syrup, and butter. Cook until butter melts. Remove from heat and add vanilla and salt. Empty sugar into bowl and pour melted butter over sugar, stir until moistened. Work smooth with hands. Work in coconut and press into buttered pan. Melt chocolate and spread over top of candy. Chill and cut into squares.

Chocolate Maple Coconut Fudge

1 cup maple sugar
1 cup brown sugar
2 tablespoons butter
¼ cup maple syrup
¾ cup cream

2 ounces or squares chocolate
½ cup shredded coconut
½ cup pecans

Mix sugar, butter, syrup, cream, and chocolate in a pan to boil. Cook to soft ball stage. Remove from burner. Add coconut and pecans. Beat until creamy. Pour into pan and sprinkle more nuts on top.

Cocoa Fondant Fudge

2 ½ cups sugar
1 tablespoon glucose
3 tablespoons butter
½ cup cocoa
½ cup milk
1 teaspoon vanilla
2 tablespoons fondant

Bring to a boil, sugar, glucose, butter, cocoa and milk. Hard boil to 240 degrees. Turn off the heat and stir in the vanilla and fondant. Beat until creamy and thick. Pour into buttered pan and mark off into squares.

Simple Chocolate Fudge

4 ounces unsweetened chocolate
1 ½ cups milk
4 cups sugar
Dash of salt
¼ cup butter
2 teaspoons vanilla

Melt the chocolate in the milk until smooth. Cook on low until mixture begins to thicken. Add sugar and salt, stirring until it boils. Boil without stirring to the soft ball stage. Remove from burner. Add butter and vanilla and stir. Leave it alone to cool. When lukewarm beat it until the mixture is no longer shiny. Pour beaten mixture into buttered pan.

Chocolate Bar Fudge

1 milk chocolate bar - 7 ounces
1 dark sweet chocolate bar – 7 ounces
1 cup marshmallow cream
1 tablespoon butter
1 teaspoon vanilla
2 cups sugar
1 cup evaporated milk
1 cup chopped pecans

Put chocolate bars in a bowl with the marshmallow cream, butter, and vanilla. In a large pan, mix sugar and milk. Bring to a boil and stir until it reaches the soft ball stage. Takes about 6 minutes. Pour hot mixture over the chocolate, stirring until well blended. Pour into a buttered pan to cool.

Cold Chocolate Fudge

2 cups powdered sugar
½ stick butter
1 egg beaten
2 tablespoons cream
2 ½ squares chocolate melted
1 teaspoon vanilla
1 cup nuts

Cream the sugar and butter together. Add the egg, cream, chocolate, vanilla, and nuts. Pour into a baking dish and chill. Cut into squares to serve.

Plain Brown Wrapper Fudge

¾ cup milk
1 teaspoon cornstarch
2 cups sugar
1 cup brown sugar
1 teaspoon vanilla
1 cup nuts

Mix the milk and cornstarch together. Add sugars, and bring to a boil. Cook to the soft ball stage. Add vanilla and nuts. Cool. Beat. Pour into buttered pan.

Caramel Chocolate Fudge

2 cups light brown sugar, packed
2 tablespoons cocoa
⅛ teaspoon salt
½ cup corn syrup
½ cup milk
½ cup evaporated milk
1 teaspoon vanilla
2 tablespoons butter
2 cups chopped pecans.

Dissolve sugar, chocolate, and salt in milk and syrup. Cook on medium heat until mixture reaches the soft ball stage. Stir occasionally. Remove from heat and cool. Add vanilla, butter, and pecans. Beat until smooth and creamy. Pour into buttered square pan.

Chocolate Butter Fudge

3 cups sugar
1 package unflavored gelatin
1 cup milk
½ cup corn syrup
3 squares of chocolate
1 ½ cups butter
2 teaspoons vanilla
1 cup chopped pecans

Combine sugar and gelatin in a pan. Add the milk, syrup, chocolate, and butter. Cook this mixture to the soft ball stage, about 238 degrees. Remove from heat and pour into a large mixing bowl. Add the vanilla and cool about 15 minutes. Beat until mixture becomes thick. Stir in the nuts and pour into a buttered pan for cooling.

Target Practice

      Miss Freda Fiddlestick moved into her new home. She found an old farm house built in the mid 1800's with ten fenced acres of tall buffalo grass. Everything was going well until she decided to buy herself a herd of goats. For a time her neighbors were skeptical that she could even do the milking. It was a funny thing to watch. The first time she tried to coax the milk from the larger nanny goat, she had very little luck. However, the next morning, the nanny had a small baby by her side and the milk flowed freely. No one had told Miss Freda that the nanny goats had to be fresh or have babies to give milk. This goat thing was an adventure she would not forget soon. Before the month was out, she had ten goats instead of only four. Two of the nanny goats had twins. She did not get much milk from them. She was happy for a while, milking the nanny goats and using the milk in her fudge.

One late afternoon, Mrs. Sammy J. Burkelheimer, the principal of Sling Shot's elementary school, came to visit and they discussed the goat business.

"My dear, you can't expect these nanny goats to simply supply your milk forever. As soon as their babies get old enough, they will no longer produce milk. You need to buy a Billy goat and put him in there with the nanny goats."

Being a city girl, Miss Freda never thought about it that way. "Hmmm, you may be right about that. Okay, that is what I need to do then. I shall have a Billy goat by tomorrow night."

The next day Miss Freda put on her finest sequined blouse and headed off to the local auction barn. She was right at home amongst all the men and was even the center of attention where usually the animals took center stage. Once the animals ran through the auction ring, Freda picked out the Billy goat she wanted and brought it home.

One afternoon later in the week, Freda was stirring up a batch of her wonderful fudge when she heard a commotion on her back porch. She ran out to see what was going on and the Billy goat had torn the screen off the back porch door and was helping himself to her pans of cooling fudge. Freda yelled at the goat to stop. It looked up and shook its head violently.

"You had better get on out of here, you hairy beast." The goat bleated loudly and pawed the floor. Freda noticed a gleam of something not so nice in the goat's eye. She turned to run and the goat charged at her. Miss Freda barely made it to the kitchen door and closed it behind her before the goat hit the door with his horns. She just knew that the goat would go back to the cooling fudge and eat until he was full. No longer would she be able to put her fudge on the back porch to cool.

Ms. Sammy came over to visit again one afternoon and Freda told her about the Billy goat's fancy for fudge.

"You know I thought it would be a good idea to give folks with sensitive stomachs a taste of my fudge. I still think it is a good idea. The only bad thing is that darn Billy goat. He eats more fudge than I can cook and he makes a target of me when I don't feed him fudge."

"Why not teach that Billy goat a lesson then?" Ms. Sammy asked her dear friend.

Shortly afterwards, Ms. Sammy became the object of target practice for the raging Billy goat. The woman took her life in her own hands when she decided to help Miss Freda. The two women herded the animals into the small pen and left the Billy goat in the back yard. Miss Freda had cooked up a batch of her famous cayenne pepper fudge with ample cayenne.

Once the fudge was ready to cool, Miss Freda sprinkled the red pepper on top of the fudge coating it thoroughly. "This ought to break that egg sucker."

"I thought he was a fudge eater. Has it been getting into someone's eggs, too?"

"Egg sucker is just an expression." Freda giggled between sprinkles. "What's the matter with you, girl, haven't you ever heard someone call something an egg sucker before?"

Ms. Sammy shook her head. "Not really. I have been in the classroom most of my life. Mostly as a student." Ms. Sammy got a faraway look in her eyes and began talking about her time in college. That was a long time ago, too, but Miss Freda listened politely.

"I'll never forget the time I had that neat professor who wore those tight white jeans. I had some of my own white jeans and he told me that he often watched me in my jeans. What he didn't know was that I watched his tight jeans, too." Ms. Sammy giggled like a schoolgirl and fluttered her lashes.

Miss Freda chuckled at her friend. "Wish I had the memory and the education you have. Furthermore, I would love to have those long beautiful eyelashes you have. But, that is another thing entirely. Let's get this Billy goat taken care of so I can have my back porch to myself again."

Miss Freda and Ms. Sammy carried the pans of fudge to the cooling racks on the back porch. The Billy goat stuck his nose in the air and sniffed. He came running and nosed right into the fudge. The cayenne pepper began its work. He bleated, ran in circles, reared up, butted the wall, and finally plopped his face into the water bucket, causing trays of fudge to spill all over the porch. When Ms. Sammy bent to pick up the spilled trays, the big Billy goat attacked her. She screamed and the neighbors came running. Her head was stuck in a large pot. In the pot was the remaining fudge Miss Freda had not poured into a cooling pan.

Ms. Sammy stumbled headlong off the porch, into the back yard where she sat down hard. The Billy goat came charging again and butted the pan on her head. It then began licking the fudge that dripped out of the pan and down her shirt.

"Call for back up from Officer Babs." Miss Freda squealed and then told everyone to beware of the Billy goat. "That animal is a menace. Stay out of his way and do not turn you back on him. Miss Freda's friends and neighbors helped her take the pan from Ms. Sammy's head. Miss Freda led her dear friend into the house to help clean her clothes and hair.

After they scraped the fudge from Ms. Sammy's head and shoulders, the Billy goat struck again.

Officer Babs turned the nanny goats out with the Billy and then herded all of them back into their pen. She shut the gate, and took a bow to the crowd.

"Be sure you wire that gate shut—".

A sudden hush fell on the crowd and Freda caught her breath. Before Officer Babs could retreat and get out of the way, the Billy goat rammed the gate and popped it open. Officer Babs sprinted as fast as a rookie, but her legs just could not outrun the raging Billy goat. He made contact with the fleshy part of Babs's backside, and she flew through the air, landing in the middle of a puddle of fudge. Her face was covered with the sticky stuff. The goat followed his target to the fudge puddle and began lapping it from Officer Babs' face. Babs threw her hands in the air laughing hysterically.

"Oh my goodness, are you hurt?" Miss Freda huffed and puffed after her dash from the back porch.

"Nothing but my pride. I thought I was doing so well, but you know something? That latch on the gate is broken."

Miss Freda nodded. "I know, that darn goat broke it the first night I put him in the pen."

Officer Babs stood up and wiped at her face where the goat had not cleaned it up. "Not bad fudge, Freda. It does have a little bit of kick to it, though."

Freda laughed. "It should. I put a whole can of cayenne pepper in it. Sure made that goat mad, too."

Miss Freda, Officer Babs, and Principal Sammy all three laughed. They had planned to teach the goat a lesson; instead, the goat taught them not to try to outwit a goat.

Relieved that Officer Babs and Ms. Sammy Burkelheimer were not injured, and grateful for all the neighbors' help, Miss Freda invited everyone inside for coffee and a fresh plate of her wonderful fudge.

The next day, Miss Freda Fiddlestick put an ad in the

paper.

Wish to sell goats CHEAP! The Billy goat will have to go to someone who leaves him in a large pasture or who can make fudge for him every day.

Chocolate Oatmeal Fudge

2 cups sugar
4 tablespoons cocoa
½ cup milk
1 stick butter
½ cup marshmallow cream
3 cups oatmeal

Mix sugar and cocoa in a pan and cook with the milk and butter. Cook to the soft ball stage, and pour over marshmallow cream and oatmeal, making sure everything is mixed well. Pour into buttered dish and cut in squares after it cools.

The Best Chocolate Fudge

2 small bags chocolate chips
1 large jar marshmallow cream
2 sticks butter
4 cups sugar
1 large can evaporated milk
1 teaspoon vanilla
1 cup pecans

Empty the chocolate chips in a bowl with the marshmallow cream. Set aside. In a large pan, mix the butter, sugar, and milk. Boil the mixture for 8 minutes until it comes to the soft ball stage. Pour the hot mixture over the chips and marshmallow cream. Mix in the vanilla and the pecans. Pour into a buttered flat cake pan and set for 24 hours.

Chocolate Bar Fudge

4 cups sugar
1 13-ounce can condensed milk
1 stick butter
12 to 15 ounces milk chocolate candy bars
1 - 7 ½-ounce jar marshmallow cream
Chopped pecans and vanilla.

Bring sugar, milk, and butter to a boil. Boil until soft ball stage. Remove from burner and add chocolate and marshmallow cream. Stir until smooth. Add chopped pecans and vanilla to taste. Pour into large buttered pan.

Millionaire's Fudge

4 cups granulated sugar
1 stick butter
1 large can milk
2 large chocolate bars
2 packages chocolate chips
1 jar marshmallow cream

Bring the first three ingredients to a boil for about 8 minutes. You had better stir it all the time or it will boil over. Into the boiling mixture, stir the remaining ingredients except the nuts. Take it off the heat and beat it well. Add the nuts just before you are ready to pour it up into a buttered pan.

Creamy Chocolate Fudge

1 ½ cups sugar
⅔ cups milk
1-6 ounce package semi-sweet chocolate chips
½ cup marshmallow topping
¼ cup margarine
½ cup chopped walnuts
½ teaspoon vanilla

Combine sugar and milk. Cook over medium heat to a full boil. Cook 10 minutes longer, stirring occasionally. Remove from heat and add the remaining ingredients. Beat until chocolate is melted and the mixture begins to thicken. Pour into buttered pan and cool.

Heavenly Fudge

5 cups sugar
1 large can milk
¼ pound butter
3 small packages chocolate chips
1 jar marshmallow cream
1 pound pecans
1 tablespoon vanilla

Cook the first three ingredients to the boil. Bring the boil to the soft ball stage. Remove from heat and stir in the remaining ingredients. Beat until smooth and pour into a well-buttered pan.

Chocolate Walnut Fudge

⅔ cups evaporated milk
1 ½ cups sugar
¼ teaspoon salt
¼ cup butter

2 cups marshmallows-cut up
1 ½ cups semi-sweet chocolate morsels
½ cup chopped walnuts

Mix the first five ingredients in a saucepan and bring to a boil. This mixture must be stirred constantly to avoid scorching. Cook on low for exactly 5 minutes from the start of the boil. Remove from heat adding chocolate. Stir this until all chocolate is melted. Add vanilla and walnuts and spread into a buttered pan to cool

Marvelous Fudge

4 cups sugar
1 can evaporated milk (14 ounces)
1 cup butter

1 package semi-sweet chocolate pieces (12 ounces)
1 pint marshmallow cream
1 teaspoon vanilla
1 cup broken walnuts

Butter the sides of a large saucepan (3 quart). Combine sugar, milk, and butter. Cook over a medium heat until mixture reaches the soft ball stage (236 degrees). Remove from heat and add chocolate, marshmallow cream, vanilla, and nuts. Beat until smooth and chocolate is melted. Pour into buttered pan and let set overnight.

Million Dollar Fudge

1 large can evaporated milk
4 ½ cups sugar
3 bags chocolate chips
2 jars marshmallow cream
1 cup pecan halves

Mix and cook the milk and sugar for 6 minutes. After it boils, take off heat and stir in chocolate chips, marshmallow cream, and pecan halves. Pour into buttered pan and cool at least 8 hours.

Foolproof Fudge

2 ½ cups sugar
⅛ pound butter
½ can – (6 ½ ounces) evaporated milk
1 package chocolate chips
1 ½ bars German chocolate cut into pieces
½ pound chopped nuts
½ pt. marshmallow cream

Stir the sugar, butter, and milk to mix well in a sauce pan. Cook until it boils for 5 minutes. Pour hot mixture over chocolate, nuts, and marshmallow cream. Mix all very well. Pour into buttered pan and cool.

Rocky Road Fudge

4 - 4 ½ ounce milk chocolate bars
3 cups miniature marshmallows
¾ cups broken walnuts

Melt chocolate in top of double boiler. Do not let the water in
bottom boil. Butter up an 8X8 inch pan. Remove melted
chocolate from the fire and beat it with a spoon until it is
smooth. Now stir in the marshmallows and walnuts and spread
in the buttered pan. Chill until firm and cut into squares.

Marshmallow Cream Fudge

2 cups sugar
1 cup whipping cream
1 tablespoon butter
10 large marshmallows, chopped

Combine milk and cream and bring to a boil. Cook until syrup
forms a soft ball when tested in cold water. Add butter and
marshmallows. Take off the heat. Beat to a thick creamy
consistency. Pour into a buttered pan.

King Mallow Fudge

1 6-ounce milk chocolate bar, plain or crunchy
2 cups miniature marshmallows
2 6-ounce packages semi-sweet chocolate morsels

Melt milk chocolate bar over hot water. Spread in greased 8-inch square pan. Sprinkle with marshmallows. Melt chocolate morsels, stirring until smooth and creamy. Spread gently over marshmallows. Chill. Cut into squares.

Marshmallow Fudge

2 cups light brown sugar
½ cup milk
1 cup marshmallows cut in quarters
1 teaspoon butter
½ teaspoon vanilla
⅛ teaspoon cream of tartar

Cook the sugar, cream of tartar, and milk without stirring until a soft ball forms when some is dropped into cold water. Cool slightly and add the marshmallows, butter, and vanilla. Beat until creamy and pour into a shallow buttered pan to cool and cut into squares. Nuts may be added if you wish.

My Marshmallow Fudge

4 ½ cups sugar
½ pound margarine
2 small cans evaporated milk
2 packages semi-sweet chocolate chips
1 teaspoon vanilla
8 ounce jar of marshmallow cream
½ pound pecans

Mix sugar, milk, and margarine and boil for 10 minutes. Remove from heat and add marshmallow cream, chocolate chips, and beat. Add pecans and vanilla. Beat until cool. Pour into buttered pan.

Sling Shot Fair Baked Goods

G.Vancil

Fair Fudge Fight

The Sling Shot Livestock Show and Fair kicked off with a bang. The baked goods judging caused a ruckus among the women of Sling Shot. The baked goods and homemakers entries outnumbered everything else. More than a thousand items needed judging. Judges included members of the local Dessert of the Week Women's Club, who did not enter the contest, and Mr. McBain, the local bakery chef along with

Miss Freda Fiddlestick. She offered her expertise as a judge in the pies and cakes because she did not enter those two categories.

"I have judged fudge before, and that can be tough, but I think this task of choosing a best cake or pie from all these wonderful confections will be quite easy." Dressed in her sequined finery, Freda preened in front of the captured audience in the small building.

Fireman Joe sauntered up to Freda looking her up and down. "Miss Freda, you look as delicious as some of those decorated cakes over there. I hear you are judging this year?"

"Well, Joe you handsome devil you, I sure am the judge and I think you might be able to sway my vote if you baked one of those wonderful pies or cakes."

"Sorry to disappoint you Miss Freda, but I don't cook. I'm here to present the blue ribbons, when you judges get done with your jobs."

Freda danced a little jig and squirmed closer to Joe. Her fudge was sure to win and to have Joe present the ribbon was the best thing in the world. She might just steal a kiss from him when her fudge won first place then best of show." Thank goodness she didn't have to judge the best of show category. Gee that man was a hunk of good looking stuff

Officer Babs stepped up to the announcer's stand and took the microphone in her hand. Her voice blasted on the airwaves. "Everyone listen up, here is her honor, Mayor Roo-Roo."

The smallish woman stood on the stage and cleared her throat a time of two before she held the microphone up to her lips. In a loud clear voice, she spoke. "Clear the area where the baked goods are displayed. The judges need room to do their jobs. We will not have you people milling about trying to get a look at the judge's scorecards. Now clear out. " Mayor Roo-Roo knew how to handle a crowd.

A 4-H student served each judge as helper, walking along behind them with a glass of water and a few soda crackers on a plate. Those students who had baked things to be judged were not allowed to help.

Miss Freda and Horace, the frizzy red-headed 6th grade boy assigned to her went down the line of cakes and pies. "This isn't as easy as I thought it was going to be. I may be sick before the night is done." She looked at the remaining half of the entries needing judged.

"Do I have to taste every one?"

"Yes ma'am, that's the rules all right."

"I really don't like the taste of some of these at all." Freda tried not to show her disgust at the taste of some of the entries, especially if the contestant used salt instead of sugar. There were two of those already, mustn't let on to the audience.

Horace just nodded, his red hair bobbing in the wind of the fans blowing in the room.

"Hmm, I suppose you're right. Here's what I'm going to do. You wait right here, I'll mark my card for good looks on these, and then I'll go back and taste the best looking ones. Let my palate rest so to speak. Wait here."

Horace waited. He watched her walk up and down the line. Each little bit she wrote something on her scorecard. After judging the appearance of the cakes and pies, she then went back to each concoction and tasted it.

"Sure is hard not to make a face when you get a mouth full of salt instead of sugar. Hand me a napkin. I think I am drooling all over my chin."

"Yes, Ma'am." Horace felt sorry for Miss Freda; she had just taken a bite of his sister's chocolate cream pie. He tried to tell her not to put salt instead of sugar in there. Nevertheless, the girl just threw her nose in the air and reached for the wrong canister. "She won't win then, will she Miss Freda."

"No I'm sorry, but not this entry." Horace shrugged. He had tried to warn Sarah, it was her own fault she didn't win. He should have cooked something to enter, like he wanted to do in the first place.

Once Miss Freda finished judging the entries, she turned in her scorecards. One cake in particular won hands down and one pie took the cake. "They must have been made by the same women." She wanted the recipe for both, but had no idea who the cook might be, probably none of the women she had met. They made such fun of their own cooking, and each was a good cook in her own field, well with the exception of Della Laverne. That girl couldn't boil water. Oh well, she would see in a few minutes.

The action in the homemaker's barn began. Chef McBain stepped up to the microphone to announce the winners. He was the closest thing to a celebrity in Sling Shot, well except for Freda Fiddlestick. She was fast becoming the most notable person. Everyone knew Miss Freda or at least knew of her fudge making skills. Her sequined blouses came in a close second to her fudge when it came to knowing Miss Freda. Her clothing always sparkled brightly.

"The winner of the cake division, judged by our very own Miss Freda Fiddlestick. I would like to present the blue ribbon to…"

"Drum roll please!" Miss Freda picked her way from the back of the crowd to the front where she could pass the blue ribbon to Joe. Being close to that man made her heart go pitter pat.

"And the winner is—Ms. Della Laverne for her eggless pineapple upside down cake. Come on up Leggie. Joe has your blue ribbon."

"I am coming, get out of the way you people. I didn't even have to call on Joe when I baked this cake. The Sling Shot Fire Department knows my house—and my cooking—far too well! " Della Laverne took the blue ribbon and kissed Joe on the cheek.

She leaned over and whispered to Freda. "I dated him one time; he isn't worth the trouble." She winked.

"Well that spoils the batter, doesn't it?" Freda whispered to Officer Babs, who stood beside her.

"I don't care if she did date him. I like him. She dated almost everyone to hear her tell it."

The women giggled and listened to the rest of the winners.

"And last but certainly not least, the winner of the candy division. My, what a pleasure to judge this competition! Yum, Yum!" Mr. McBain announced. "Who else, but our very own fudge queen, Miss Freda Fiddlestick wins first, second, third, fourth, and fifth place. That's all the ribbons we had for the candy division, or there would have been more. You have been a busy lady Miss Freda,"

"Thank you so much." Freda preened in front of the crowd waiting for Joe to hand her the ribbon. She was ready for the presentation. She intended to see if Leggie's words were true.

Joe, in his fire chief's hat handed her the ribbon, but before Freda could lay her lips on his, Ms. Harvey came rolling down the aisle. At least it looked like she was rolling. Her legs were too short for her to look like she was walking.

103

"I am contesting this win. My Susie had an entry in that category and her fudge was excellent this year. I demand you change your decision."

"Ms. Harvey, fudge is not to be eaten with a spoon, but rather with one's hand, or a fork from a plate. Your daughter's fudge was not set up properly and therefore didn't win."

"My mother made her fudge to be eaten with a spoon as far back as I can remember and her mother before her did too. You, sir, are not the expert on fudge making and I say you are not a fair judge of fudge."

"Ms. Harvey, I didn't spend all those years in culinary school for nothing. I do have a diploma saying that I am a certified chef, and I do believe I am capable of telling if fudge is properly set or not."

Ms. Harvey slowly removed her glove, "I say you are not. Our fudge recipe has been handed down from generation to generation and I say it is the winner. Now are you going to retract your decision or not?"

"Not!"

"Very well, then" Ms. Harvey scooped a hand full of her daughter's fudge entry and smushed it into Mr. McBain's mouth. "I believe that is called eating fudge with one's hand or another one's hand.

Appalled that the judge's decision was being second-guessed, Freda made a quick decision to participate in the discussion. "Ms. Harvey, Mr. McBain is right. Fudge is not supposed to be eaten with a spoon. I've been making fudge for several years and have won many ribbons with my fudge." About the time she started to continue, Ms. Harvey shoved a hand full of fudge into Freda's mouth.

Freda spat the sugary concoction out and quickly held her hand out. Joe, being a proper gentleman, slapped a handkerchief into her hand. She wiped her mouth and face free of the syrupy mess.

"I am usually not a violent person Ms. Harvey, but you asked for this." Freda stuck her hand into the runny fudge and gave Ms. Harvey a taste of the chocolaty confection.

From that point on, the adults of Sling Shot lost control of themselves.

Officer Babs trying to stop the mêlée blew her whistle, but the noise fell on deaf ears. Finally, she took the bullhorn, blasted over the crowd in her best police voice, "I said to cease and desist." Officer Babs surveyed the room. Not one pie or cake was left on the tables. Several people were holding their eyes or cheeks where they had been pelted with bread loaves. Dishes lay broken into chards. Jelly and jam was scattered all over the floor, but somehow Freda Fiddlestick's fudge came out of the fight intact.

The brand new hat Ms. Harvey ordered from a Paris catalog would never be the same. Its bright red and blue ostrich plumes were speckled with fudge and other sweets. Mr. McBain's toupee hung above his ear on one side, dripping with chocolate

"I will never judge this women's category at this fair or any other ever again. I would rather judge the hogs and step in the poop than to set foot in this homemaker's barn as long as I live. I would much rather get in a snake pit full of snakes at the rattlesnake roundup than to deal with these neurotic women of Sling Shot."

"Now Mr. McBain. Let by-gones be by-gones. If Ms. Harvey will apologize, you will judge again, won't you." Officer Babs tried to straighten things out so there were no hard feelings.

Freda still clean but for the tiniest bit of sugary syrup on her forehead, offered Mr. McBain and the town folks a

105

chunk of fudge instead of a spoonful. Her first place confections appeased the angry women whose baked goods lay destroyed on the floor of the homemaker's barn.

Trying to place the toupee back on his head, Chef McBain moved back to the lectern. "Miss Freda your fudge saved the day. I proclaim you Fudge Queen of Sling Shot."

Roo-Roo's Favorite Fudge

4 ½ cups sugar
1 can of milk
2 cups nuts
2 sticks butter

3 small bags chocolate chips
3 tablespoons vanilla

Bring sugar and milk to a boil. Cook for 6 minutes stirring constantly. Pour over nuts, chips, and butter. Mix well and add vanilla. Pour into buttered dish.

Avi Nell's Chocolate Fudge

2 cups sugar
1 cup milk
½ teaspoon salt
2 squares unsweetened chocolate
2 tablespoons light syrup
2 tablespoons butter
½ teaspoon vanilla
½ cup nut pieces

Mix sugar, milk, salt, chocolate, and syrup in a pan and bring to a boil over low heat. Cook stirring occasionally so as not to stick. When the mixture reaches the soft ball stage, remove it from the heat and drop in the butter. Do not stir until the mixture cools to lukewarm or 110 degrees. Add vanilla and beat until mixture loses its shiny consistency. The candy should begin to hold its shape. Stir in the nut pieces and pour into a buttered dish to cool.

Bernie Lee's Fudge

2 cups evaporated milk
1 cup white syrup
6 cups sugar
6 squares chocolate
½ pound butter
2 teaspoons vanilla
2-3 cups pecans

Bring to a boil, the milk, syrup, sugar, and chocolate. Stir constantly to the soft ball stage. Remove from heat and add butter. Do not stir. Let it stand until you can touch the bottom of the pan. Add vanilla and beat until mixture holds its shape. Add nuts and pout into buttered pan.

Gwenella Rose's Brown Fudge

2 cups sugar
4 cups sugar
2 cups cream
1 tablespoon corn syrup

½ cup butter
¼ teaspoon soda
1 teaspoon vanilla
2 cups pecans

Caramelize 2 cups sugar. While sugar is cooking, combine remaining sugar, cream, and syrup in another pan. Boil to soft ball stage. When sugar is caramelized, pour in a thin stream into the boiling mixture. Stir it constantly. Cook to firm-ball stage. Remove from heat and add butter and soda. Stir until melted. Cool before adding vanilla. Beat until thickened. Add pecans and pour into a buttered pan.

Lazy Man's Fudge

2 cups sugar
¾ cup milk
2 tablespoons chocolate
2 tablespoons white syrup
1 teaspoon vanilla
2 tablespoons butter

Boil all together until it forms a soft ball when tested in ice water. Remove from heat and beat until thickened. Pour into buttered dish.

Oil Baron's Fudge

4 ½ cup sugar
1 large can evaporated milk
3 packages chocolate kisses
1 jar marshmallows crème
2 sticks butter
4 cups chopped pecans

Mix sugar, milk, and butter. Bring to a boil. Boil 10 minutes on low heat. Remove from heat. Add marshmallow crème, kisses, and pecans. Drop on wax paper by spoonfuls.

Rich Man's Fudge

3 cups brown sugar
½ cup half and half
¼ cup butter
¼ cake of chocolate

Melt chocolate. Add milk, butter, and sugar Bring to a boil for
about 9 minutes or to the soft ball stage. Cool in buttered pan.

Mammie's Million Dollar Fudge

4 ½ cups sugar
2 tablespoons butter
Pinch of salt
1 can milk
12 ounces chocolate chips - semi-sweet
12 ounces German sweet chocolate chips
1 jar marshmallow cream
2 cups chopped pecans

Boil sugar, salt, and milk for 6 minutes. Put chocolate chips,
marshmallow crème, butter, and nuts in a bowl. Pour the hot
mixture over them and beat until all is melted. Pour into
buttered pan and let set for 24 hours before cutting into
squares.

Freda's Favorite Fudge

⅔ cup evaporated milk
1 ⅔ cups sugar
16 large marshmallows
1 ½ cups chocolate chips
1 teaspoon vanilla
½ cups chopped nuts

Combine milk and sugar in pan over medium heat. Bring to boil, cook 5 minutes, stirring constantly. Remove from heat and stir in marshmallows, chips, vanilla, and nuts. Beat until marshmallows are melted. Pour into buttered pan.

Law Dawg Fudge

1- Pound chocolate candy bar
2 packages chocolate chips
2 cups nuts, chopped
1 bottle marshmallow crème
4½ cups sugar
1 large can condensed milk
⅔ stick butter

put the first four ingredients into a bowl and set aside. Stir sugar, milk, and butter until it comes to a rolling boil. While stirring, cook for 5 minutes. Pour over the first four ingredients until all the chocolate is melted thoroughly. Pour into a large baking pan and chill.

Aunt Bell's Brown Fudge

2 cups sugar
4 cups sugar
2 cups cream
1 tablespoon corn syrup
½ cup butter

¼ teaspoon soda
1 teaspoon vanilla
2 cups pecans
2 packages butterscotch chips

Caramelize 2 cups sugar. While sugar is cooking, combine remaining sugar, cream, and syrup in another pan. Boil to soft ball stage. When sugar is caramelized pour in a thin stream into the boiling mixture. Stir it constantly. Cook to firm-ball stage. Remove from heat and add soda. Stir in butter and chips until melted. Cool slightly before adding vanilla. Beat until thickened. Add pecans and pour into a buttered pan.

Aunt Sarah's Fudge

3 cups sugar
2 squares unsweetened chocolate
1 cup table cream
1 tablespoon butter
1 teaspoon vanilla
1 cup chopped pecans

Cook ingredients together without stirring until they form a soft ball when dropped in water. Cool and beat until creamy. Add chopped nuts and vanilla. Pour onto a buttered dish and cut into squares when cool.

Robyn Etta's Delicious Pecan Fudge

2 cups sugar
1 cup firmly packed brown sugar
2 cups whipping cream
1 cup light syrup
1 teaspoon vanilla
1 cup chopped pecans
1 cup pecan halves

Put the first four ingredients in a large saucepan and bring them to a boil. Stirring constantly, boil for about 9 minutes or until a small amount dropped into ice water forms a soft ball. Take it off the fire and cool it without stirring. After it is cool and the pan can be touched without burning the flesh, beat the fudge until it thickens and loses its glossy texture. Add vanilla and chopped pecans to the mixture. Pour into a buttered pan and decorate with the pecan halves.

Mabel's Fudge

4 large chocolate candy bars
1 cup salted cashews
 1 jar marshmallow cream
1 package chocolate chips
4 cups sugar
4 teaspoons butter
1 can evaporated milk

To begin with, put sugar, butter, and milk in a pan and start it to cooking. Bring it to a boil and boil it hard for about 7 minutes. This needs to be stirred all the while it is boiling. The candy bars, cashews, chocolate chips and the marshmallow cream can be put into a bowl and when the mixture is done at 7 minutes, pour it over the ingredients in the bowl. Mix all and pour into a buttered pan. You can beat it to make it cool down and start to thicken or just leave it alone and it will set up, it takes a lot longer if you do not beat it.

Babs's Mocha Fudge

¾ cup evaporated milk
3 tablespoons instant coffee
2 ½ cups sugar
1 jar marshmallow crème
¼ cup butter
1 package semi-sweet chocolate chips
1 teaspoon vanilla

Put the milk and coffee in a large heavy pan and make sure the coffee dissolves. Add the sugar, marshmallow crème, and butter. Bring to a boil and stir constantly. Over medium heat boil for about 7 minutes. Beat in the chocolate chips and vanilla until it is all well blended. Pour mixture into greased square pan.

Della Laverne's Chocolate Fudge

1 pound brown sugar
2 cups sugar
3 squares chocolate
1 teaspoon vanilla
2 tablespoons corn syrup
⅓ cup half and half
¾ cups cold water
¼ teaspoon salt
1 cup chopped nuts

Combine sugars, chocolate, corn syrup, cream, water, and salt. Cook slowly to soft ball stage. Remove from heat and allow to cool undisturbed until pan is cool to touch. Stir until creamy adding vanilla and nuts. Pour into and spread in a buttered pan. If it gets too stiff to pour into pan, pour it out onto a buttered surface and knead like bread dough until it becomes soft and elastic then put into pan to set up.

Flower Pan's Fudge

5 level tablespoons cocoa
⅔ cups water
2 cups sugar
⅔ cups milk
2 level tablespoons butter
1 teaspoon vanilla

Mix sugar and cocoa together thoroughly. Add milk and water then cook until a drop or two of the mixture makes a soft ball when dropped into cold water. Stir occasionally to keep it from sticking. When done add vanilla and butter. Put pan in a larger pan of cold water and stir until the mixture forms a ball. Nuts may be added at this time.

Neighbor Bill's Buttermilk Fudge

2 cups sugar
3 squares chocolate
¾ cups buttermilk
⅛ teaspoon cream of tartar

3 tablespoons butter
1 teaspoon salt
1 teaspoon vanilla
12 marshmallows

Stir well the sugar, chocolate, and milk. Let it come slowly to a boil, keep sauce pan well covered until it boils. Add cream of tartar and salt. When it forms a soft ball in water, add the butter and marshmallows. Remove from fire and beat well until creamy. Add vanilla. Beat a few minutes and pour into well-oiled pans. Mark into squares.

Joe's Chocolate Fudge

1 ⅓ cups milk
4 ounces chocolate
4 cups sugar
2 tablespoons white corn syrup
½ teaspoon salt
¼ cup butter
4 teaspoons vanilla

Melt chocolate and butter over low heat. Stir in the sugar, syrup, and salt. Cook over a medium heat bringing the mixture to a boil. Stir constantly to a soft ball stage. Remove from heat and cool to lukewarm without stirring or jarring the pan. Add the butter and vanilla. Beat until the mixture turns dull then turn it into a buttered pan. Set to one side to cool.

Bubba's Chocolate Fudge

2 ½ cups sugar
4 heaping tablespoons cocoa
½ cup light cream
½ cup light syrup
A pinch of salt
1 teaspoon vanilla
1 lump of butter the size of an egg
1 cup fresh pecans

Cook all except vanilla, butter, and pecans until it forms a soft ball when dropped into cold water. Take it off the heat and stir in butter, pecans, and vanilla. Let it stand for 15 minutes. Beat until it begins to thicken. Pour out on wax paper and cut into squares.

Sammy's Strawberry Fudge

3 cups sugar
4 tablespoons Strawberry gelatin dry
⅛ teaspoon salt
¾ cup milk
½ cup cream
1 tablespoon white syrup
2 tablespoons butter
1 teaspoon vanilla
1 teaspoon strawberry extract
¼ cup finely chopped nuts

Mix the first 6 ingredients in a heavy sauce pan. Bring to a boil and cook to the soft ball stage. This takes about 8 -10 minutes of boiling on medium heat. Do not stir. Remove from heat. Add butter and extracts, but do not stir until the outside of the pan is lukewarm. Stir things up adding nuts and beating until the fudge loses its glossy consistency.

Phoebe's Fudge

2 cups sugar
¼ cup butter
½ cup canned milk
3 – 6 ounce packages chocolate chips
2 cups marshmallow crème
1 cup nuts
1 teaspoon vanilla

Cook sugar, butter, and milk to soft ball stage, about 10 minutes of hard boiling. Take it off the fire and add the rest of the ingredients. Beat it until it is not shiny anymore. Pour into a buttered pan and let it cool.

Diva Devine's Buttermilk Fudge

2 cups sugar
3 squares bitter chocolate
¾ cups buttermilk
1/16 teaspoon cream of
tartar

3 tablespoons butter
1 teaspoon salt
1 teaspoon vanilla
12 marshmallows

Stir well the sugar, buttermilk, and chocolate. Let it come slowly to a boil, keeping sauce pan well covered until it boils. Add cream of tartar and salt. When it forms a soft ball in water, add the butter and marshmallows. Remove from fire and beat until creamy. Add vanilla and beat a few more minutes. Pour into a well-oiled pan and mark off into squares.

Granny's Buttermilk Fudge

2 cups white sugar
1 cup buttermilk
2 tablespoons white syrup
1 teaspoon soda
½ stick butter
1 cup nuts

Mix first four ingredients and bring to a boil in a large pan. Add butter and cook to a soft ball stage. Let cool. 15 to 20 minutes. Beat until it loses its gloss and pour into pan. Cut into squares.

Mo's Chocolate Fudge

2 cups sugar
½ teaspoon salt
2 squares of semi-sweet chocolate
1 cup evaporated milk
2 teaspoons butter
½ teaspoon vanilla

Cook sugar, salt, chocolate, and milk slowly until sugar
dissolves, then cook rapidly to soft ball state, stirring often.
Cool. Add butter and vanilla. Beat until thickened and turn out
onto buttered plates and mark.

Uncle Jack's Chocolate Fudge

2 cups sugar
1 small can milk
80 mini marshmallows or 10 large ones
1 stick butter
¾ teaspoon vanilla
1 small package chocolate chips
Pinch of salt
1 cup nuts

Cook sugar, milk, marshmallows, vanilla, salt, and butter in heavy saucepan for about 6 minutes. Put chocolate chips in large bowl and pour hot mixture over all. Beat until well blended and creamy. Either drop by spoonful on wax paper or pour into buttered pan and cut into squares.

Mom's Chocolate Fudge

2 sticks margarine
4 cups sugar
1 large can evaporated milk
2 small packages chocolate chips
1 large jar marshmallow cream
1 cup nuts

Pour chocolate chips and marshmallow cream into mixing bowl. In a saucepan, mix the sugar, margarine, and milk. Boil for 9 minutes. Pour hot mixture over chips and marshmallow cream. Beat until no longer glossy. Pour into buttered pan and cut into squares when cool.

Dad's Favorite Chocolate Fudge

2 cups granulated sugar
1 cup milk
½ teaspoon salt
2 squares unsweetened chocolate
2 tablespoons white corn syrup
2 tablespoons butter
½ teaspoon vanilla extract
½ cup broken nut meats

Combine sugar, milk, salt, chocolate, and syrup in pan over low heat. Stir until sugar melts. Cook to 238 degrees stirring constantly to prevent sticking and scorching. Remove from heat and mix in butter; do not stir. Set to one side until it cools to the touch. Add vanilla and beat until the mixture is no longer glossy looking. It should be holding its shape by this time. Fold in the nuts and pour into a buttered pan to finish cooling.

Jerry's Favorite Fudge

2 cups sugar
¼ cup cocoa
¼ cup corn syrup
¾ cup milk
Vanilla to taste

Put all ingredients into saucepan and boil to soft ball stage.
Pour into buttered pan. Cool and eat.

Aunt Pearl's Fudge

4 cups sugar
¼ pound butter
2 cups less 2 tablespoons half & half cream
2 small bags milk chocolate chips
3 ½ cups marshmallow pieces
1 cup nuts

Boil cream, sugar, and butter to the soft ball stage. Combine
chocolate chips, nuts, and marshmallows in a large mixing
bowl. Pour the boiling sugar mixture over the chips mixing
quickly. Do not beat. Spread into 2 square pans that have been
buttered. Chill. Fudge will keep for several weeks if kept in
covered dish in refrigerator.

Funeral Parlor Fudge

"I can't believe that Miss Bernie Lee is gone. Why, just yesterday she gulped down a batch of my fudge and coffee, sitting right here at this very table." Freda Fiddlestick shook her head and popped a piece of fudge into her mouth.

"I know Freda. It seems like just yesterday I was fixing her hairpiece for her. She was talking nonsense about not being here much longer, I thought she was going on a trip." Diva Denny didn't fix hair much anymore. Only for a select

127

group would she stand behind someone with a comb and brush. Her expertise shone in the written word or an artists' brush.

"Miss Bernie Lee was the founding mother of the Dessert of the Week Club, you know. It's still Sling Shot's most renowned women's club. She was only twenty-two the year she decided that a new dessert each week would keep a body healthy."

Freda popped another square of fudge in her mouth and sipped her coffee.

"Were you one of the ninety-six women who joined her club back then, Sue Roo-Roo? What about you, Gwenella?"

The women shook their heads. "Nope, neither one of us like to cook. We didn't join because you had to know how to cook and bring a new dessert each week to the meetings."

"I never made a decent dessert in my life." Della Laverne chimed her two cents in the conversation. "In fact I hardly ever turn my stove or oven on. Either event calls for the Fire department. I dated them one time, you know."

Freda wanted to ask Della Laverne who baked the winning cake from the fair, but this was neither the time nor the place.

"I've heard that." Ms. Sammy J. Burkelheimer snickered.

"Well, all I can say is she must have been right about the desserts being healthy. The newspaper says she lived to be one hundred and twelve years old. She didn't look a day over eighty. Of course, at eighty, she didn't look a day over fifty. Heck, we all thought it was because she was married to a plastic surgeon. She was a fine woman." The women all nodded in agreement.

Freda caught a sarcastic look from Della Laverne. "She recently turned over the mantle of command of the Dessert Club to you, didn't she Freda? I believe she told everyone that, and I quote, 'Miss Freda Fiddlestick has the right attitude about life. Be young, wear gaudy sequins and earrings, and cook great desserts.'"

"Why yes, Della Laverne, you got her words perfect this time." Ms. Sammy J. spoke up. The last thing needed was a fight in the funeral parlor.

"The last attribute being the most important, I believe that's what Miss Bernie Lee said. Freda never shies away from acting young, wearing gaudy sequined clothes, or earrings. I have known her only a few months, but I am impressed with the way Freda directed traffic too." Della Laverne added a bit of a sneer that Miss Bernie Lee hadn't ever had in her voice.

"And she like the way Freda directed a parade." Officer Babs walked into the funeral parlor and joined the women's conversation.

"I think Miss Bernie Lee was envious of the way Freda became known as the Fudge Queen of Sling Shot. Miss Bernie's attention turned to Freda here from the beginning."

Freda spoke softly of her friend. "Miss Bernie and I became fast friends after only a few chance meetings. Of course every time I visited her at the Singer home for the elderly, I carried a fresh batch of fudge."

"Is that why Miss Bernie left you in charge of her estate?"

Freda looked white as a ghost. "She did not!"

"Yes, she did." Flower Pans chimed in. "I heard the funeral director tell her nephew you were the one in charge of everything except the services. I have to take care of all that stuff. She and I were friends before some of you were even born."

Freda held her hand over her mouth as she choked on the coffee she sipped. "Well that's a fine thing to do to a friend, isn't it? I wish she had told me what she was doing, I

129

would have told her to leave Officer Babs or Robyn Etta in charge. They are both more qualified than me."

"Miss Bernie's dessert club members prepared everything. The deceased's instructions and wishes are being carried out even as we all sit here and talk about her."

"I wonder if her ears are ringing." Avi Nell's whispered too loudly. "She sure planned things out. I think that's great, that way no one had to do anything but follow directions. I like that."

Freda stood to look in on the casket where her friend lay. She popped another square of fudge in her mouth and chewed slowly. She listened to her friends as they discussed the woman lying in the next room.

"The Dessert Club cookbook recipes were followed closely, I can tell you that for sure." Flower Pans' quiet voice took on a glow as she remembered the woman who would never eat fudge again.

"Folks who attend the funeral will be invited to the Baptist Church afterwards for desserts, and Freda has prepared more than 200 recipes of fudge for the occasion."

"Two hundred?"

"Yes, over two hundred. That was at the request of the deceased." Flower Pans spread her arms to show the fudge. "She loved Freda's fudge. Didn't she Freda?"

"Yes, she loved every one of the fudges I ever made for her."

The women all looked at the batches of fudge placed around the parlor room. Some of the plates were nearly empty and others still stacked high with fudgy squares of candy. Others had only a few pieces gone.

Soon the funeral director called everyone to the chapel and the women, all officers in the Dessert of the Week Club except Mayor Roo-Roo and Gwenella Rose sat together like a

130

small family in the family pews with only a nephew and Fireman Joe with them. Joe had been a fifth cousin twice removed in a round-about way.

The service went as most services did. The pastor got up and said a few words about Miss Bernie Lee and everyone cried. The Club members rose and sang three songs for Miss Bernie. There was not a dry eye in the house when the pastor stood to finalize everything with a prayer. Once he said "'Amen'". A loud crashing pop resounded throughout the chapel. People jumped from the pews and ran for the outside door. Even the Dessert of the Week Club members did not sit still. The Pallbearers ran for the side door. The funeral turned into pure chaos.

Once everyone was out of the church, all afraid they were about to meet their own maker, Fireman Joe began searching for the reason of the noise.

"Don't worry folks, I'll find out what's going on around here."

"I think Miss Bernie Lee's trying to get the last word in. She always did have to have things her way." Officer Babs, not one to be overly emotional, ventured back toward the chapel first, followed by the rest.

Joe ran from behind the church. "I found cause of the explosion. That big old gorilla balloon the car lot uses to advertise its new deals just burst. The percussion from that blew out some light bulbs in the church. There are chunks of brown fudge-colored rubber all over the place. See." He held a large slice of brown rubber for all to see.

The mourners muttered about how the deceased might have ordered the explosion of that giant gorilla, meandered back into the church where Miss Bernie Lee lay smiling in her custom-made fudge-colored casket. Each member of the Dessert club grabbed a chunk of fudge off the plates on the tables, as they passed the casket. It had been ordered, that everyone eat a chunk of Freda's fudge as they viewed the body.

"Could be she did set the whole thing up to happen just this way, too." Freda determined Miss Bernie's send-off would not fall short of a record for the most delicious and frightening funeral in the state gathered up the plates of fudge and hurried inside. She passed the plate like a good Baptist and urged everyone to take a piece of fudge. "This is to celebrate the most delightful person who ever lived in Sling Shot."

As the fudge ran low, she hurried out of the chapel to where Frankenstein sat, and pulled pans of fudge from every nook and cranny of the old vehicle. She even brought her experimental versions. Fudge made with jalapenos and various other vegetables went fast. The first to disappear were the zucchini and avocado batches.

Comments from the funeral participants sending Miss Bernie home were heartwarming. One comment in particular came up time after time. "I sure am going to miss Miss Bernie, but the legacy she left in her Dessert Club will probably live a long and delicious life in the capable hands of Miss Freda Fiddlestick with her wonderful fudge recipes."

The pastor of the Baptist church ended the ceremony with the deceased's final announcement. "Miss Bernie Lee would like to invite all of you to the church fellowship hall where she instructed her club to serve you, her friends through the years, all the desserts you can eat."

Almond Fudge

4 cups sugar
2 tablespoons golden syrup
1 cup milk
1 teaspoons salt
1 tablespoon vanilla
¾ cups chopped almond

Place sugar, syrup, milk, and salt in a deep pan. Bring the mixture to a good rolling boil. Hold the boil until the mixture makes a soft ball when dropped into cold water. Remove from heat. Add vanilla and almonds. Beat the mixture until it begins to thicken. Pour into buttered dish.

Walnut Brown Sugar Fudge

1 cup light brown sugar
1 cup sugar
¾ cup milk
1 tablespoon butter
1 teaspoon vanilla
½ cup walnuts

Cook the sugars and milk in a saucepan until it reaches the soft ball stage. Remove from heat and add the butter and vanilla. Cool and beat until very thick. Add walnuts and pour into a buttered pan. Set in refrigerator.

Butterscotch Nut Fudge

¼ cup butter
1 cup brown sugar
1 cup sugar
¾ cup sour cream
1 teaspoon vanilla
½ cup chopped almonds

Melt butter and add brown sugar. Add sugar and sour cream.
Cook to the soft ball stage. Cool without stirring. Beat until
mixture holds it shape and is smooth. Add vanilla and almonds.
Pour into buttered dish.

Buttermilk Nut Fudge

2 cups sugar
2 tablespoons light syrup
1 cup buttermilk
2 tablespoons butter
1 teaspoon soda
1 cup nuts
Pinch of salt
1 teaspoon vanilla

Cook all ingredients except vanilla and nuts to the soft ball
stage. Stir constantly. Remove from heat and beat until creamy
and smooth. Add vanilla and nuts. Pour into buttered dish. Cut
in squares to serve.

Butterscotch Pecan Fudge

1 package butterscotch pudding
½ cup brown sugar
½ cup evaporated milk
1 cup sugar
1 ½ cup chopped pecans
1 tablespoon butter
1 teaspoon vanilla

Combine all ingredients and bring to a boil. Cook for 5 minutes beating constantly. Remove from heat. Beat until thick. Pour into buttered dish.

Black Walnut Fudge

3 squares of unsweetened chocolate
2 cups sugar
2 tablespoons corn syrup
½ cup cream
2 tablespoons butter
1 teaspoon vanilla
½ teaspoon baking powder
½ cup black walnuts

Boil the chocolate, sugar, syrup, butter, and cream until it forms a soft ball in cold water. Remove from burner add vanilla and baking powder. Beat until smooth and creamy. Add the black walnuts and pour into a buttered pan to cool. Cut in squares to serve.

Chocolate Nut Fudge

3 cups brown sugar
½ cup half and half
¼ cup butter
¼ cake of chocolate
1 cup pecans

Melt chocolate. Add milk, butter, and sugar Bring to a boil for about 9 minutes or to the soft ball stage. Cool a little, adding nuts and beat until thick and smooth. Pour into pan and allow to set overnight.

Pinon Fudge

3 cups sugar
13 ounces evaporated milk

1 teaspoon vanilla
½ cup Pinon nuts

Melt 1 cup sugar in a heavy pan. Stir only with a wooden spoon until the sugar is dark brown in color. Add the remaining sugar and stir in the milk gradually. Cook to hard ball stage and remove from heat. Add vanilla and beat until creamy. Fold in the nuts and pour into a buttered pan. Cool and cut into squares.

Nutty Fudge Frosting

3 squares unsweetened chocolate, cut in pieces
1 ½ cups milk
3 cups sugar
Dash of salt
3 tablespoons light corn syrup
3 tablespoons butter
1 ½ teaspoons vanilla
1 cup chopped pecans may be added, if desired.

Cook chocolate and milk over low heat until mixture is smooth
and blended, stirring constantly. Add sugar, salt, and syrup, stir
until mixture boils. Continue cooking, without stirring, until a
small amount of mixture forms a soft ball when dropped into
cold water. Remove from fire. Add butter and vanilla. Cool to
lukewarm. Beat until of spreading consistency and pour into
buttered pan. When cooled cut into squares.

Becca D's Chocolate Nut Fudge

3 cups sugar
3 squares chocolate
½ cup light corn syrup
1 cup milk
4 tablespoons butter
1 teaspoon vanilla
1 cup chopped pecans

Cook sugar, chocolate, corn syrup and milk over low heat stirring constantly, until mixture reaches soft ball stage. Remove from heat and add butter. Cool to lukewarm and add vanilla. Beat until creamy and smooth then stir in pecans. Beat until it begins to thicken. Pour into buttered pan.

Butter-Pecan Fudge

5 tablespoons butter
1 ¼ cups brown sugar
1 ¼ cups sugar
1 cup sour cream
1 teaspoon vanilla
1 cup pecans chopped

Melt the butter in a heavy pan. Add the brown sugar and heat to boiling. Add sugar and sour cream. Cook until all sugar is dissolved and it reaches the soft ball stage. This must be done on low heat. Cool until slightly warm to the touch. Beat the mixture until it is stiffened. Add vanilla and pecans and spread into a buttered pan to cool

Chocolate Almond Fudge

1 cup brown sugar
1 cup sugar
¼ cup corn syrup light or dark
¼ cup butter
½ cup half and half
2 or more squares chocolate
2 teaspoons almond extract
1 cup slivered almonds

Combine sugars, syrup, cream, butter, and chocolate. Cook until mixture is tested in cold water and forms a soft ball. Take it off the heat. Put in the almond extract and beat it until it becomes stiff. Add the almonds and pour into a slightly buttered pan.

Coconut Fudge Too

3 cups sugar
2 tablespoons corn syrup
3 squares bitter chocolate
⅛ teaspoon salt
1 cup evaporated milk
1 cup flaked coconut
1 cup nuts chopped
3 tablespoons butter

Place all ingredients except the nuts and butter in a saucepan and boil until the temperature reaches 240 degrees. This should be the soft ball stage. When a small amount of the sugar mixture is dropped into a small amount of cold water, there will be a soft ball of sugar form. Remove from heat and add butter. Stir until it melts. Beat mixture until it is creamy. Add nuts and coconut then pour into a buttered pan or roll the mixture into a roll and wrap in plastic. When cool either cut into squares or slice off the roll.

Creamy Pecan Fudge

2 cups sugar
⅔ cups milk
2 tablespoons corn syrup
2 squares of chocolate
2 Tablespoons butter
1 teaspoon vanilla
1 ½ cups pecans

Cook sugar, milk, syrup, and chocolate in a sauce pan until it comes to a boil. Boil to 236 degrees. Remove from heat and add the butter stirring until it melts. Cool fudge lukewarm and add the vanilla. Beat until fudge loses its glossy appearance. Stir in pecans and pour into buttered pan.

On the Road with Fudge

Freda Fiddlestick opened the memory book and thumbed through the pages. "Ah memories. Aren't they sweet?"

"I love to look back at where I've been and see all the pictures of the past come alive again." Officer Babs got that starry-eyed look on her face. It was the same look she got when Joe came around.

"Me too," Robyn Etta sighed.

"Who are those ladies, Freda?"

"Oh them, they're the ladies who got me started cooking up fudge. I met them in Eureka Springs, Arkansas when I drove old Frankenstein to the Ozarks. Lovely place. Lovely women, too." Freda reached back into her archives and told the story of her trip.

"Franky and I were on the road again. I would sometimes get the urge to travel and since I hadn't seen any of the great nation we live in, I just drove. Where I ended up, no one would know for sure. I like to drive and Franky just took me where the wind would blow us. That year I ended up in the Ozarks. Eureka Springs was the most beautiful place you ever saw. That's where I met these two dames. That's what they call themselves. They make the best fudge you ever ate, well except mine of course."

"You do make good fudge Freda." Babs reached for another piece.

Robyn Etta agreed.

"Well these women were just getting started; they were still cooking fudge in the basement of one of their homes. I couldn't believe it. Man that was one nice setup. I thought they were really dumb to be cooking so much fudge in their basement. Told them so too, after we got to be good friends. Anyway, that's what they named their company."

"What? Really Dumb Fudge?"

"Naw, Two Dumb Dames Fudge."

"They didn't get mad at you?"

"No, they laughed and told me I was a genius because I gave them the name of their fudge company. Anyway, we were friends by then. Friends are supposed to be able to tell each other if they are dumb or do stupid things, aren't they?" Freda popped a chunk of fudge in her mouth.

"I tell you one thing, they can make that fudge. I especially love their pumpkin fudge and they make the best melt in your mouth milk chocolate fudge you ever slapped a lip around." Freda reached for another square of chocolate fudge.

"Where else have you been Freda. Gosh, I bet you have been everywhere. I've hardly been out of the state." Officer Babs looked at Freda wistfully.

"Well, I went to Paris once."

"Paris, France?"

"Don't I wish, no, Paris, Texas. Nice little town, but I didn't stay long. Nothing for me there. I did go to New York with some friends one Thanksgiving. We did that town up right, too. Let me tell you. We did all the regular touristy stuff. You know the Statue of Liberty, the subway, the Macy's parade. All that stuff." Freda flipped through the pages of her album and showed them the pictures of her New York adventure."

"I can't believe you went to New York." Robyn Etta stuffed a chunk of fudge in her mouth and sipped her coffee. "I love this combination, Freda. This coffee fudge and the coffee together really make it neat tasting."

"Thank you. That is my own invention. I stumbled onto it quite by accident one morning when I first got here to Sling Shot."

"I remember that morning. That's the day of the unexpected parade with no permit." Babs cleared her throat and grinned at Freda.

"Well, yes, I believe it was, speaking of parades. Here are the pictures of the Macy's parade I took. Lovely parade. Such nice folks in New York, too. I was prepared for the worst when I arrived, but never saw such nice people. My friends were from Texas and we all wore cowboy hats so we could keep up with each other. It is quite a large city."

Her friends laughed are her seriousness.

She shrugged her shoulders. "Anyway, the day of the parade, my friends abandoned me for the TV. It was so cold and they all stayed at the hotel room to watch the parade while I braved the cold and the elements to sit in the grandstands. It was a dream of my mother's to go and watch that parade. She never got to go, so I went and did it for her or in her memory.

"However, the bus went off and left me behind, so I had to walk a ways before I could find a cab. Besides, you can see so much when you walk around a town. I found the neatest little fudge shop there and bought some of it for my friends. They loved it. They loved the story about the yellow roses too. I bought them at a rose boutique. Beautiful place, roses everywhere you looked and remember this was in November. I went in there thinking I would just buy myself a rose. I don't have anyone to buy roses for me. So I went inside and I couldn't count the number of different varieties those folks had in that tiny little spot. More than on Miss Bernie Lee's old bushes. I picked up several different ones, and then I decided that since my friends were all from Texas and I was living there at the time, I might just as well buy yellow roses for each of them. I like for people to remember me. You know, like the lover off to war remembers his girlfriend. Everyone needs to be loved."

Miss Freda wiped a tear from her cheek.

"Anyway, I ordered six yellow roses. I wanted one too. Wouldn't you know it though; the lady at the store didn't have but five roses that were just alike in yellow. I whined around a little and finally she found me six rose buds all in yellow. Beautiful flowers. So I grabbed one of those yellow cabs and back to the hotel on Broadway Street I went with my roses. When I got back to where my friends were, they had all been shopping too. They bought yellow roses for all of us to share, just like I did. Isn't that neat. That is the story of my New York trip."

"Tell us more about your travels, Freda."

"Not much else to tell. I've been to New Mexico several times, not much out there but shrubs and cowboys. Got some nice looking cowboys out in Clovis and Roswell. Even saw the funny lights out in West Texas near Marfa. Read a book about haunted forts in Texas. The lights of Marfa are portrayed as ghosts. Who knows? Then I've been to Corpus Christi and looked out over the beach with a few friends I met a long time ago. Even tried to drive the ferry on the water there. That's a breeze to get to and it is really beautiful there. I looked out over that ocean and I imagined it was nothing but fudge. The white caps on the waves look like divinity fudge and I get so hungry. One dear friend that lives there, she knows all the best places to find out of the way food joints too. Love it."

"I've been to Shreveport, you know, just up the road a piece. Love the casino life there, but Frankenstein got jealous because I stayed in the big hotels instead of keeping him company. Then it was down there to Opelousas where we had wine and cheese. That's where I found another book on haunted forts of Louisiana. It's by the same author as the other haunted forts book. That woman really did some traveling to get that research on those two books. I found one more of her books just recently too. I was looking for cookbooks and there it was big as life, a book on frontier foods. The lady knows her business about food. It was after I got to looking at that book I decided what I wanted to do with my life."

Babs took a bite of fudge before asking, "What is it you want to do with your life Freda, write about your escapades?"

"Well, I do have a journal, but no, actually, I want to open up a fudge factory." I think I would be really good at it and I love to cook fudge."

"How did that frontier foods book make you think you wanted to cook fudge the rest of your life?"

"Well, it's like this. I read about those frontier women, how they cooked, and how they must have felt. I bet they felt as if they were in a rut and maybe they wanted out of the rut. Well, I'm in a rut and I love to cook, I love to make fudge. So why not?"

Babs tried to tie the book and the fudge factory together, but somehow Freda's reasoning didn't gee-haw. Oh well, she did make good fudge. "So what will you call your fudge factory when you get it?"

"Haven't made up my mind yet. I've been toying with ideas, but none sound right."

Robyn Etta turned the page on the picture album and squealed. "Why not name it after this photo?"

"Which one is that?" Freda took the book away from her friend and looked at the backsides of four friends.

"Why not indeed." Freda beamed "Fat Fannies Fudge Factory. It'll be perfect! Now if I could just win a lottery somewhere."

Quick Peanut Butter Fudge

¼ cup butter
½ cup creamy peanut butter
1 pound powdered sugar
½ cup powdered milk
½ cup corn syrup
1 tablespoon water
1 teaspoon vanilla
½ cup nuts

In a double boiler, melt the butter and peanut butter. Stir in the syrup, water and vanilla. Stir in dry ingredients after being sifted together. Make sure all ingredients are mixed thoroughly. Remove from heat and stir in nuts. Pour into greased or buttered pan.

Quick Bean Fudge

1 cup cooked pinto beans
¼ -½ cup milk
1 teaspoon vanilla
6 ounces unsweetened chocolate
6 tablespoons butter
2 pounds powdered sugar
1 cup nuts or raisins optional

Mash together the first three ingredients. Should resemble mashed potatoes. In the meantime, melt butter and chocolate in a double boiler. Pour the chocolate over the beans. Stir until thickened. Add sugar and nuts or raisins. Get your hands in it and knead smooth. Spread in a little buttered pan and refrigerate.

Flea Market Fudge

1 16-ounce jar chunky peanut butter
1 container of vanilla frosting (any brand)

Mix these two ingredients together and pour it into a buttered pan. Put this in the refrigerator and allow it to set up. Easy and fun to make. Tastes great. Can use milk chocolate frosting.

Quick Chocolate Fudge Roll

½ cup butter
3 ounces unsweetened chocolate
1 pound box powdered sugar
½ cup instant milk
½ cup corn syrup
1 tablespoon water
1 teaspoon vanilla
½ cup nuts
½ cup miniature marshmallows cut into pieces
½ cup finely chopped nuts

Melt chocolate and butter in double boiler. Stir in the syrup, water, and vanilla. Sift together the instant milk and sugar. Add to chocolate mixture blending well. Mix in nuts and marshmallows. Pour onto waxed paper and roll. Sprinkle finely chopped nuts on the roll and wax paper. Cover the fudge roll with the nuts. Chill and slice to serve.

Five-Minute Fudge

1 large chocolate bar
1 large bag small
marshmallows
2 cups pecans
1 large can milk

2 packages chocolate chips
4 ½ cups sugar
3 tablespoons butter

In a bowl mix chocolate bar, marshmallows, pecans, and chocolate chips. Mix sugar, butter, and milk in saucepan and bring to a boil. Boil 5 minutes. Pour hot mixture over ingredients in bowl. Beat until thick and pour out onto a cookie sheet to cool.

Magic Fudge

1 cup semi-sweet chocolate
chips
½ stick butter
1 package Magic Frosting
Sugar

1 teaspoon vanilla
⅓ cup evaporated milk
¼ teaspoon salt
1 cup chopped pecans

Melt chocolate chips and butter over hot water in a double boiler. Mix sugar, vanilla, milk, and salt in a bowl until smooth. Add melted chocolate and butter stirring until blended. Add nuts and quickly spread into buttered square pan. Chill 30 minutes and store in refrigerator.

Lazy Day Fudge

12 ounces chocolate chips
¾ cup sweetened condensed milk

Melt the chocolate chips in a double boiler. Remove from heat and stir in the milk until it is well blended. Spoon the mixture into a square brownie pan and chill until set. Cut into squares to serve.

Quick Fudge

2 6-ounce packages semi-sweet chocolate chips
¾ cups sweetened condensed milk
1 teaspoon vanilla

Melt chocolate chips in double boiler. Remove from heat. Stir in milk and vanilla. Mix until well blended. Pour into pan and allow to cool. Cut into squares.

Quick Chocolate Fudge

¼ cup butter
3 squares chocolate-unsweetened
½ cup light corn syrup
1 tablespoon water
1 teaspoon vanilla
1 pound powdered sugar
½ cup chopped nuts
1 cup miniature marshmallows

Melt chocolate and butter over low heat. Add syrup, water, and vanilla. Remove from heat and add powdered sugar, nuts, and marshmallows. Stir until well blended and smooth.

Blonde Fudge

¼ cup butter
½ cup light syrup
2 teaspoons vanilla
1 pound powdered sugar
½ cup nuts
1 cup marshmallows

Melt butter and syrup. Remove from heat and add vanilla, powdered sugar, nuts and marshmallows. Stir until all is melted and smooth. Cool until set.

Brown Sugar Fudge

¼ cup butter
½ cup dark corn syrup
½ cup brown sugar firmly packed
1 teaspoon vanilla
1 pound powdered sugar
½ cup chopped nuts
1 cup marshmallows

Melt brown sugar and butter together with vanilla and syrup.
Remove from heat and add remaining ingredients, stirring until
smooth and creamy. Cool uncovered.

Peanut Butter Fudge Fast

¼ cup butter
½ cup crunchy or creamy peanut butter
½ cup light corn syrup
1 tablespoon water
1 teaspoon vanilla
1 pound powdered sugar
½ cup chopped nuts
1 cup miniature marshmallows

Melt peanut butter and butter over low heat and add syrup, water and vanilla. Remove from the heat and add the powdered sugar, nuts, and marshmallows. Stir until well blended and smooth. Pour into pan and cool before serving.

5+2-Minute Fudge

⅔ cup evaporated milk
1 ⅔ cups sugar
½ teaspoon salt
1 ½ cups diced marshmallows
1 ⅔ cups chocolate chips
1 teaspoon vanilla
½ cup chopped nuts.

In a saucepan, over low heat, bring to boiling the sugar and milk. Cook for 5 minutes. Remove from heat. Add remaining ingredients and stir for another minute or two at least until marshmallows melt. Pour into buttered 9-inch pan and cool.

Fast and Fabulous Fudge

3 tablespoons butter
⅔ cup evaporated milk
1 ½ cups sugar
½ cup white syrup
1 8-ounce package of semi-sweet chocolate chips
2 cups miniature marshmallows
1 teaspoon vanilla
Chopped nuts

Combine the butter, milk, sugar, and syrup. Stir constantly cooking over medium heat to a full rolling boil. Cook for five minutes. Remove from heat. Add chocolate chips marshmallows, vanilla, and nuts. Stir vigorously for one minute or until chocolate and marshmallows are melted. Pour into pan and chill in the refrigerator until firm. Takes about an hour.

Two-Minute Fudge

1 pound powdered sugar
½ cup cocoa
⅛ teaspoon salt
¼ cup milk
1 teaspoon vanilla
½ cup butter

Combine all ingredients except butter and mix as well as you can. The mixture will be too thick to totally mix the ingredients. Put the butter in the bowl on top of the dry mixture. Microwave all ingredients on high for two minutes. Remove and stir or beat until smooth. Pour on wax paper lined pan and chill for 1 hour.

Microwave Fudge

1 box powdered sugar
½ cup cocoa
1 cup pecans, chopped
¼ pound butter
2 tablespoons vanilla

In Microwave safe bowl, dump in everything except vanilla and nuts. Microwave the ingredients on high for two minutes. Stir in vanilla and nuts, pour in buttered pan and chill for at least an hour.

Sinful Fudge

1 pound powdered sugar
½ cup cocoa
1 stick butter
¼ cup milk
1 tablespoon vanilla
1 cup pecans

Add all ingredients in order except nuts and do not stir.
Microwave on high for 1 ½ - 3 minutes melting the butter. Stir
in nuts and mix well. Pour into buttered pan and cool.

Holiday Fudge

2 pounds powdered sugar
2 cans milk
2 tablespoons butter
½ teaspoon salt
2 small packages semi-sweet chocolate chips
6 tablespoons marshmallow cream
1 teaspoon vanilla
2 cups chopped nuts

In a saucepan put the sugar, milk, butter, and salt. Bring this to a boil for 4 minutes. Remove from the fire and add chocolate chips and marshmallow cream. Beat until chocolate melts and the mixture begins to thicken. Add the vanilla and nuts before turning it into a buttered pan to cool

Quick Walnut Fudge

4 ½ cups sugar
⅓ pound butter
1 can milk
3 packages chocolate chips
1 pint jar marshmallow cream
2 cups chopped walnuts
2 teaspoons vanilla

Boil the first three ingredients to the softball stage and pour over the remaining ingredients. Stir all together until melted. Do not beat. Pour into a buttered dish and let it cool.

Easy Fudge

1 package chocolate pudding mix
¼ cup butter
1 ½ cups sifted powdered sugar
¼ cup chopped nuts
¼ cup milk

Put the pudding mix, butter, and milk into a saucepan and bring
to a boil. Boil for one minute. Keep stirring it. Remove from
heat and stir in sugar making sure it is all blended. Add the nuts
and pour it into a greased pan. Wrap in plastic wrap to keep it
soft and creamy.

Kissing Fudge

4 ½ cups sugar
1 can evaporated milk
2 packages chocolate candy kisses
1 pint marshmallow cream
2 cubes butter
2 teaspoons vanilla
2 cups hazelnuts chopped

Mix sugar and milk and boil it for 9 minutes. Do not let it scorch. Pour over the remaining ingredients and mix. Pour into a buttered dish.

No Cook Fudge

2 packages milk chocolate chips
¼ pound marshmallows
1 can sweetened condensed milk
1 cup chopped pecans

Melt the chocolate and milk together. Pour over the marshmallows and nuts. Drop by spoonful onto waxed paper.

Quicker 'n' That Fudge

3 cups sugar
2 tablespoons white corn syrup
1 cup milk
4 tablespoons cocoa
1 tablespoon butter
1 cup chopped pecans

Mix all ingredients except butter and pecans. Cook to softball stage then add butter and pecans. Beat until thick (only takes a few minutes). Pour into greased platter or pan.

Frankenstein Retired
from Service

Miss Freda pulled up in front of the local domino hall in Sling Shot. It served as the Dessert of the Week Club meeting place on Mondays. She sounded the horn. Her friends ran out the door from their meeting oohing and awing over the new minivan she drove.

"Where did you get this beauty?" Officer Babs ran her hand over the golden paint job. "And when did you get home? We've missed you."

"Just got home last night, late. Wait until I tell you all what happened to me."

"This is beautiful Freda, but what did you do with Frankenstein. Don't you think he'll be jealous?"

Freda threw her hands in the air to call time out. "Wait a minute. First things first, I'm here to invite you all to my house this evening for fudge and drinks. I've already alerted Gwenella and Mayor Roo-Roo. Make it about fiveish." She climbed back into the new van and fired up the engine. "See, no backfiring or wheezing or anything. By the way, this is Bride of Frankenstein. I call her Brunhilda. Isn't she a beauty?" She patted the door of the van.

Freda stepped on the gas pedal and roared down the street, leaving her friends standing with mouths agape.

At a little after four o'clock, the women started arriving. Officer Babs was the first.

"I had a run in the neighborhood and thought I'd see if you needed any help or anything."

"Come on in." Freda held her hand out for Babs' cap and hung it on the hat rack with her vintage collection.

"Why don't women wear hats anymore? I think women in hats are so feminine and somewhat romantic too. Don't you?"

Babs nodded. "Uh huh. Hey, why did you get a van?"

"You sure aren't one to hem-haw around are you, Babs?" Freda grinned at her friend.

Just as she was about to tell Babs to wait for the rest of their friends, a knock resounded from the front door.

"Babs, be a darling and plug in the coffee pot. I don't think I should wait any longer."

A look of disappointment crossed Babs's face and she turned to plug in the coffee pot. Then she began carrying the cups and saucers to the table.

No sooner had Freda ushered Diva Devine and Mayor Roo-Roo to the kitchen, the doorbell at the back door rang.

168

Minutes later, Ms. Sammy Burkelheimer, Avi Nell's, Robyn Etta, and Flower Pans trooped into the kitchen following Freda.

"I'm coming in the front door. Don't anyone shoot me!" Gwenella Rose made her way to the kitchen table, picked up a chunk of fudge, and popped it into her mouth. "Mm, the most delicious vegetarian thing I have eaten all day. Now what's this I hear about a new van?"

The others laughed at her. Gwenella Rose was a beauty and such a kid at times, just like a little gecko.

Being the hostess with the mostest, Freda flitted from the bar to the sink to the table and back to the bar. Each of her friends stood or sat at the table wishing she would hurry and tell them her wonderful news.

Babs broke up the chatter. "Spill the beans, Freda. We want to know what's going on right now. You have kept us in suspense long enough."

"I can't tell you anything. We're not all here yet."

Ms. Sammy looked around and counted. "Nope, we're not all here yet. What time did you tell us? I forgot."

"I said fiveish."

"A groan went up from the group. "What time is it now?"

"About fifteen until five."

Another groan filled the room.

"Don't worry; I'm sure you can wait. Maybe Della Laverne won't be late this afternoon."

"Do gnats have butts?"

"She'll be late."

"She'll be on time. Maybe. Anyway, have some more fudge, there's plenty. And pass that coffee pot around."

The phone rang.

"Maybe that's her."

169

"Not likely, she isn't that courteous." They all nodded as Freda went to answer the ringing phone.

Babs' detective mind registered something peculiar. Freda was not on her good phone. She was talking on one of those new-fangled cellular phones. Since when did folks in Sling Shot need cellular phones? Shoot, most everyone lived within hollering distance. Besides, Freda had never been one to be so frivolous with money. There was something mighty fishy going on in this house. Babs stepped closer to the hallway.

"All right then. Hammerhead, I'll see you in about an hour."

"Hammerhead?" Babs whispered. Who in the world was Hammerhead?

Freda came out of the hallway smiling and nearly knocked Babs off her feet. "So sorry, what are you doing standing way off over here? Have I got a surprise for you all! Wait; is Della Laverne still not here?"

"Here I am. Here I am. You'll aren't going to believe what happened to me on the way over here."

"You're late."

Leggie looked at her watch. "Oh, I am not, it is just twenty minutes after five. Freda said about fiveish. Twenty minutes after five is some sort of record for me. Anyway, like I said, you are never going to believe what happened..."

"Shh, we want to hear what happened to Freda." Avi Nell's wasn't bashful about telling people to shush when she wanted to listen to someone talk.

Della Laverne stared at Avi Nell's, but she clamped her mouth shut and sat in the closest chair.

Officer Babs broke the silence. "The floor is yours Freda, literally and figuratively. Spill your guts."

Freda in her red sequined blouse took center stage in her own kitchen. "As you all know, I went to Corpus Christi,

170

Texas to visit a friend last month. You know I told you about her. Miss Patty Pooper. She knits those prayer shawls you all liked so well. Anyways, now she is learning to make jewelry. I went down to take her some beads and yarn and have a wee visit."

"Get on with it Freda, we don't have all night. Thanks to some people, who are never on time."

Della Laverne got a defiant look in her eyes and started to protest, but Freda went on with her explanation. "While I was in Texas, I got a wild idea."

"So what else is new?" Della Laverne had to get her two cents in the conversation.

"Patty Pooper and I talked about my idea and we came up with a neat plan as to how I could start my own Fudge Factory. I was on my way home to put the plan into action when Frankenstein broke down. That's what took so long for me to get home. I had to have the old boy put in the truck hospital. It was tough for a while. Well, I had to get a nine-to-five in order to pay the bills for Franky. I went to work at a Git 'n' Go store. They sold the lottery tickets, and I won the lottery."

Freda clapped her hands together and looked at them. "Isn't that great!"

They sat with their eyes bulging and no words coming out of their mouths.

"How wonderful for you, Freda!" Robyn Etta hugged Freda then the rest of the group cheered, yelled, and grabbed their friend.

"That's how I got Brunhilda and that's why I have been gone so long. I never knew how much paperwork went into winning two hundred million dollars. I still…"

They all stopped talking and stood like statues.

"How much did you say you won?"

171

"Oh that. Two hundred million dollars, before taxes, lawyer fees, you know all that stuff had to come out of the jackpot first."

"Oh well, gee, I could handle two hundred million dollars." Della Laverne sat back in her chair, envy oozing from every pore of her being as she scarfed down a piece of fudge.

The doorbell rang and Freda left her friends to talk it all over as she opened the door. "Mr. Hammerhead. Come in please. I think you're just in time. I was about to spring my surprise on my friends."

"Just about to? Just ABOUT to? I thought the lottery bomb you dropped was a surprise." Flower Pans, always so proper, giggled softly.

"Well, yes, that was a bit of a surprise. However, I have a better one. You know I bought a new van, and a few minor things I needed, but I have one more surprise. This is for you all. Mr. Hammerhead, will you explain to these women what I've done?"

The short balding man cleared his throat and began mumbling.

"Speak up. We can't hear you."

"I said you ladies are now full and equal partners in the fudge making business. Miss Freda Fiddlestick has purchased the largest building in Sling Shot besides the city hall/jailhouse and has furbished it with everything needed to make and distribute fudge."

"Miss Fiddlestick has commissioned me to look after the paperwork and legal aspects of the company. Anyone not wishing to be a part of this is welcome not to sign these papers and that share will be divided among the rest accordingly."

"Where do I sign? I'm not bashful about things like this." Mayor Roo-Roo stepped up to the table and signed on the X.

"What's the name of the fudge place going to be? We can name it the Della Laverne Fudge Company."

"Nope, I have that all figured out." Freda pulled an eight by ten photo from a folder. "We are going to call it FAT FANNIES FUDGE FACTORY and this is going to be our logo." She held the picture of four women standing looking out to sea, bottoms up for all to see."

The ten women all signed their X and Mr. Hammerhead assured them he would file the papers first thing the next morning. As he walked out, he heard a great cheer. He listened closer as they toasted each other, leaving Freda till last.

"Now here's to Freda Fiddlestick."

"No, really," Freda spoke softly. She pulled out a tube of papers and unrolled them, holding them down on the tabletop by placing a bowl of fudge on each corner. Her friends recognized the old thrift store they had loved and hated to see closed earlier in the year. It was transformed in the pictures to a grand showroom for fudge. In the center was a pillar and on top of it was a drawing of a tired old panel truck that could only be Frankenstein, resting under a laurel wreath as the center of attention.

"Here's to Frankenstein. May he rest in retirement. If not for his breaking down this one last time, we'd still be in the poor house!"

Mr. Hammerhead looked in the screen door and saw Miss Freda, her cup held high and tears pooling in her eyes for her friend.

"To Frankenstein!"

174

Peppermint Fudge

2 tablespoons butter
1 ½ tablespoon water
½ teaspoon salt
¾ pound of marshmallows
1 small package chocolate chips
½ teaspoon vanilla
¼ teaspoon peppermint
1 cup chopped walnuts

Melt butter. Add water, salt, and marshmallows. Stir until marshmallows are melted. Bring to a boil and cook for about two minutes Remove from heat and add chocolate. Stir till chocolate is melted. Add the vanilla and peppermint. Beat until it begins to thicken. Add nuts and pour into buttered pan.

Boston Cream Fudge

1 cup white syrup
3 cups sugar
1 cup sweet cream (half & half works)
1 cup pecans
1 teaspoon vanilla
3 squares bitter chocolate
1 teaspoon butter

Bring the sugar, syrup, and cream to a soft ball stage. Remove from heat and cool until warm enough you can touch the pan. Beat until white and smooth. Stir in nuts and flavoring. Pour into buttered pan. Melt chocolate in a double boiler. Add the butter and stir well. After fudge has cooled, top with the chocolate. This needs to stand at least 24 hours or more before cutting into squares.

Christmas Butter Fudge

4 cups sugar
2 cups milk
1 stick butter
¼ teaspoon salt
1 teaspoon vanilla
¼ cup chopped candied cherries
¼ cup salted pistachios

In a large pan, mix together the sugar, milk, butter, and salt.
Bring these to a rolling boil on medium heat. Stir constantly.
Cook to approximately 238 degrees or the soft ball stage. Take
the pan and place it in a sink of cold water to cool the candy
mixture. When cooled, add vanilla and beat until it is thick and
creamy. It will not be shiny. Add the cherries and nuts and
fold them in gently. Pour into buttered pan and cool then cut
into squares.

Brown Sugar Fudge Too

2 tablespoons butter
2 cups brown sugar
¼ teaspoon slat
¾ cup light cream
¾ cup coconut
¾ cup pecans

Melt butter. Add sugar, salt, and cream. When sugar is dissolved, bring to a boil. Reduce heat and boil to soft ball stage. Remove from heat. Do not stir until cool to the touch. Beat until smooth and creamy. Add coconut and pecans. Put into buttered pan.

Molasses Fudge

1 cup brown sugar
1 cup sugar
3 tablespoons molasses
½ cup cream
¼ cup butter melted
2 squares chocolate
1 ½ teaspoons orange extract
¼ cup angelica chopped

Combine sugar, molasses, and cream. Dissolve and bring to a boil. Boil three minutes stirring constantly. Add chocolate and boil five more minutes. Remove from the heat. Add extract and angelica. Stir until candy begins to thicken. Pour into a buttered pan.

Whipped Cream Fudge

3 cups brown sugar
3 cups milk
½ cup butter
Pinch of slat
½ square chocolate, broken in pieces
1 cup whipped cream
1 cup chopped pecans
1 teaspoon vanilla

In a saucepan, put the sugar, milk, butter, salt, and chocolate. Blend well and boil hard to the soft ball stage. Remove from heat and whip with a whisk for three minutes. Add the whipped cream and beat well. Add nuts and vanilla. Beat until nearly cold then pour into buttered pan to finish cooling.

Louisiana Fudge

2 cups sugar
2 squares chocolate
⅔ cup cream
2 tablespoons corn syrup
2 tablespoons butter
2 teaspoons vanilla
Pinch of salt

Mix sugar, chocolate, cream, syrup, butter, and salt. Stir until sugar is dissolved and heat slowly. When sugar is dissolved, cover and bring mixture to a boil. Cook to 240 degrees. Add vanilla and cool. Beat until creamy and no longer shiny. Dump into a buttered pan.

Caramel Fudge

3 cups sugar
1 cup cream
⅛ teaspoon soda
4 tablespoons butter
1 tablespoon vanilla
1 cup pecans

In one heavy saucepan mix one cup of sugar and cream. In a second heavy saucepan, put remaining sugar. Cook both on low heat. Stir sugar constantly until it turns to a light brown syrup. Do not allow cream and sugar to boil yet. Add brown syrup to cream and sugar slowly. Stir it vigorously so the cream doesn't curdle. Cook until mixture forms a soft ball when tested in cold water. Take off heat and add soda, mixing thoroughly. Add butter and stir it in until well blended. Cool 20 to 30 minutes. Add vanilla and beat until thick and it loses its shine. Add nuts and pour into pan.

Caramel Chocolate Fudge
2 cups light brown sugar firmly packed
2 tablespoons cocoa
⅛ teaspoon salt
½ cup white syrup
½ cup evaporated milk
½ cup whole milk
1 teaspoon vanilla
2 cups chopped pecans
2 tablespoons butter

Stir up sugar, chocolate, and salt. Add syrup and milk. On medium heat, stir until boiling begins. Lower heat and cook until mixture forms a soft ball in cold water. Careful occasional stirring may be done. Remove from heat and cool about 10 minutes. Add butter, vanilla and pecans. Beat until gloss disappears. Pour into buttered pan and cool then cut into squares.

Maple Rich Fudge

2 cups sugar
1 cup Maple syrup
½ cup half and half
¼ cup butter

Mix milk, butter, syrup, and sugar. Bring to a boil for about 9 minutes or to the soft ball stage. Cool a little and beat until thick and smooth. Pour into pan and cool.

New Orleans Fudge

1 cup chocolate chips
1 cup butterscotch chips
1 can sweetened condensed milk
1 cup chopped walnuts
½ teaspoon vanilla
1 cup walnut halves

Melt chips with milk over hot water. Remove and add vanilla. Blend well. Chill until thickened. Butter pan and put walnut halves in pan. Pour chocolate mixture over walnuts and spread in pan. Sprinkle chopped walnuts on top of chocolate.

Maple Divinity Fudge

1 cup Maple syrup
2 cups brown sugar
1 cup corn syrup
2 egg whites
1 teaspoon maple extract

Cook sugar and syrups until crisp in cold water. Pour hot syrup mixture over stiffly beaten egg whites. Continue beating until the mixture losses its glossy texture. Add flavoring. Pour into buttered pan.

"Oooooh" Fudge

2 cups sugar
1 small can evaporated milk
12 large marshmallows
2 teaspoons French Vanilla creamer
2 tablespoons water
½ cup pecan pieces
¼ pound butter
1 ½ cups white chocolate chips
3 tablespoons vanilla

Dissolve the creamer in the water. Bring to a boil, the sugar
and milk. Over low heat, boil this mixture for about 8 minutes.
Add the creamer water to the marshmallows in the top of a
double boiler. In a large bowl, put the butter, chips, and vanilla.
Add the marshmallow mixture to the sugar and milk and then
pour over the chips and vanilla. Let it cool then beat it until it is
thick enough to hold its own form. Fold in pecan pieces.
Refrigerate until it hardens.

Christmas Fudge

3 cups sugar
¼ teaspoon cream of tartar
¼ teaspoons salt
1 cup light cream
1 tablespoon butter
1 ½ teaspoon vanilla
⅓ cup chopped pecans
½ cup chopped dates
¼ cup each green and red candied cherries

Combine sugar, cream of tartar, salt, and cream in a large heavy pan. Cook over low heat until sugar is completely dissolved. Keep sides of pan cleaned with s small amount of cold water. Bring the mixture to a boil and do not stir until it reaches the soft ball stage. Take it off the burner and drop in the butter. The mixture should not be stirred until it is cooled. Add the vanilla and beat it until it begins to hold its shape when dropped on a dish. Add the cherries and dates and stir, immediately must be poured into buttered pan. Press cherry halves on top of the candy and cut into squares to serve.

Persian Fudge

1 can sweetened condensed milk
1 cup sugar
2 tablespoons butter
1 cup pecans
½ cup prunes chopped fine
1 tablespoon vanilla or almond extract

Put sugar and milk in a saucepan and cook slowly, stirring constantly. Brown the milk and sugar slightly. Add butter, extract, nuts, and prunes. The mixture will be thick enough to spread into a pan for cooling.

Fudge For Fun

2 cups sugar
1 cup milk
2 tablespoons heaping of cocoa
2 tablespoons of white syrup
⅓ stick margarine

Combine all ingredients. Cook until soft ball stage. Remove from heat and beat, beat, beat, and beat. Pour into buttered brownie pan.

Celebrity Fudge

3 cakes of German sweet chocolate
2 cups semi-sweet chocolate chips
2 cups marshmallow cream
2 cups chopped nuts
4 ½ cups sugar
⅛ teaspoon salt
2 tablespoons butter
1 can evaporated milk

Break the German chocolate into pieces and put into a bowl with chocolate chips and marshmallow cream. Stir together the sugar, milk, salt, and butter. Bring to a soft ball boil. Takes about 6 minutes. Pour sugar mixture over the chocolate. Stir until chocolate is well melted. Add nuts. Pour into greased pan 13X9 inches. Cover tightly until it sets up and cut into squares.

GLOSSARY

Corn Syrup – use the light corn syrup unless stated otherwise. If the recipe simply calls for corn syrup, use the light. Dark corn syrup has a bolder flavor and will alter the flavor of your candy.

Cream – some of the recipes call for cream, Freda will use half and half from the dairy case.

Evaporated Milk – That is the milk that comes in the can, but look before you buy, don't use filled milk in these Freda recipes. It just doesn't do as good as the evaporated milk.

Hard Crack stage – Again, if you use a thermometer, it is marked at the proper temperature. If you are testing it in cold water, when the hot candy mixture hits the cold water, it will crackle and it is like spun glass.

Margarine, butter and oleo – these can all be interchanged in the recipes that Freda makes. Sometimes she even uses butter flavored shortening, but not often.

Marshmallow cream – don't melt your marshmallows in the candy unless the recipe calls for it. Just buy the little jars of marshmallow cream and be done with it. Some brands put out a seven ounce jar and others an 8 ounce jar, either is fine in most of the recipes.

Milk Chocolate chips – These chips do not have as much color in them as the semi-sweet and they have milk and more sugar.

Semi-sweet chocolate chips – most common in stores. Using these, the candy doesn't turn out to be too sweet and the candy is darker in color.

Softball stage – If you use a candy thermometer, it is marked off at certain temperatures for the softball state. However, Fred uses the cold water method to determine if the candy is at the correct stage of cooking. Softball stage is when you drip a few dollops of candy into cold water; you can form a soft ball with the candy.

Stirring Constantly – It means just what the words imply, stir it without stopping. Freda likes to have the radio on while she cooks and that way, she can dance to the beat of the music and stir at the same time. This gives her a full body workout, the upper arms get worked out from stirring and the dancing works her legs, hips, and waistline.

Sweetened Condensed Milk – This is sort of like evaporated milk with lots of sugar already in it.

Don't interchange evaporated and sweetened condensed milk. Now there are several brands of this sweet milk, but they are basically all the same, so use the brand you like, or better yet, make you own.

Vanilla – the extract of the vanilla bean. Freda usually uses white or clean vanilla. White or dark makes no difference unless you are making white chocolate candy. It is up to you.

About the Author

Award winning author, Elaine Laird Coleman is a sixth generation Texan. She has been writing since her elementary years making up stories and writing papers for school.

Cooking has always been a passion for Elaine and this book shows her funny side as well. *FAT FANNIES FUDGE FACTORY* is her take on over 200 recipes of fudge and cute incidents that could happen on the way to starting a business.

Elaine's last book was *CARL HALL: I DID IT MY WAY*. This book chronicles the life of spur maker Carl Hall of Comanche. It is funny and it shows the man's artistry in making bits spurs and even saddles. Read about Carl Hall and look at his work in the pages of this book.

WALT RAMBO: TEXAS STYLE BITS AND SPURS is about a man who spent 35 years as the head of the complaint department for Texas Education Association.

Her first book, *TEXAS HAUNTED FORTS* was published in 2001 with the Republic of Texas Press and she hasn't stopped writing and selling since that time.

Her third book, *LOUISIANA HAUNTED FORTS* came out in the fall of 2005 right before Katrina hit the coast.

TEXAS FRONTIER FOODS, her take on a diary and recipes passed down from an ancestor attests to Elaine's ability to report history as well as to weave an interesting tale to go along with the history of our land and foods.

Once Elaine and her husband moved to Winters, Texas, to her historical family farm she has kept her eyes and ears open for new ideas. Elaine is forever working on something new so keep your eyes peeled for her next work.

You can reach Elaine at questor@tylertel.net to request current order information.

www.ingramcontent.com/pod-product-compliance
Lightning Source LLC
Chambersburg PA
CBHW051825090426
42736CB00011B/1656